Helen Keller's Teacher

by MARGARET DAVIDSON

Illustrated by WAYNE BLICKENSTAFF

SCHOLASTIC INC.
New York Toronto London Auckland Sydney Tokyo

ISBN 0-590-02224-5

32 31 30 29 28 27 26 25 24 23   5 6 7 8 9/8

Printed in the U.S.A.   **28**

To Kit with love

Contents

A One-way Journey
to Somewhere

I'M GOING AWAY — TODAY. I don't know where and I don't care. I'm going a-a-waa-y . . . today!" The words filled Annie like a song.

In just a few minutes — surely it couldn't be longer than that — she was going to ride away in a carriage. She hugged herself. And then a train! Oh, glory!

The plans for this day wouldn't sound like much to most people. Annie knew this. But then they'd had their rides in carriages, trips on trains. Not Annie Sullivan. Only once had she felt the thrill of speed, of wheels rumbling under her, of horses running ahead. And that had been to the cemetery on the day of her mother's funeral.

1

Today would be different.

Annie didn't know where she was going, exactly. But she didn't care much. She knew it was further than the next town of Westfield, which was only five miles away. Once, long, long ago, she'd been there with her father.

No, today's trip would be much longer . . . so far that she'd never come back. That was it. She didn't know where she was going. It was a one-way journey to somewhere. But she knew she'd never be coming back here. That was the real secret glory of this day.

Annie looked around her. From where she sat on the front-porch step she could see a nice enough farmhouse, painted all clean and white. And the red barns out back, with their smell of slow-curing tobacco leaves.

But this wasn't her home. It was just a house she stayed at — a house that didn't welcome her. The people inside didn't want her — not Annie Sullivan, whose mother was dead and whose father was a drunkard. No. These people were her cousins, but they didn't want her.

They were doing their duty by her, and Annie would be happy to get out from under the weight of it. Now. Today.

But she wouldn't be going anywhere unless that carriage came. Where was it? Annie peered down the road till everything became a big blur in front of her eyes.

2

She knuckled first her left eye, then her right. Sometimes that helped. It helped this time. Annie could see a bit further now. But the road stayed empty.

"I'll close my eyes and count to a hundred. When I open them, it'll be here," Annie decided.

She began to count. Very slowly, for Annie wasn't too sure of her numbers. And if she got a number out of place, or skipped one, she'd have to go back to the beginning. That was the rule.

Seconds later Cousin Statia came banging through the front door. "There you are!" she snapped. "Where have you been all this time? I've been looking for you since breakfast."

"Twenty-three, twenty-four, twenty-five . . ." Annie continued to count. For a split second her cousin's voice had distracted her. But only for that second. Then Annie stopped listening. It was easy enough to do. Statia hardly ever said anything worth listening to anyway.

"I want you to be good today — all day. Is that too much to ask, Annie?"

Annie didn't answer. But then Statia didn't expect answers, not from Annie.

"Though the thought of your being quiet and well-behaved for an entire day . . . . At least no tantrums. Hear?

"And Jimmie . . . Annie I want to talk to you about your brother. He's little, and Ellen says his hip is no better. So you've got to fetch and carry for him — get him water and things.

"And another thing . . . Annie, we're family, and goodness knows used to your ways, but if you talk ugly with Mr. Thomas, the nice man who's come all this way to take you to . . ."

For a hairbreadth of time Statia's voice faltered. Annie didn't notice. ". . . to the train," Statia continued in a rush. "He's a stranger, and I'll die of shame if you misbehave in front of him. And also . . ." Statia's voice dripped on.

Annie counted. Cousin Statia talked. And they were both so busy listening to themselves that they didn't hear the sound of horses' hooves coming up the road.

"Ninety-eight, ninety-nine, one hundred!" Annie's eyes popped open. And there was the carriage, pulling to a stop in front of the gate.

"It worked!" Annie whispered.

"Annie, Annie, Annie! Here I am!" A little boy's head appeared through the window of the carriage. Annie paid no attention.

"Annie!" he screamed again. Annie heard him. She didn't bother to answer. She hadn't seen her brother for months, not since the family broke up. But at this moment the carriage was so exciting it demanded full attention.

A man came up the porch steps. At the same moment Cousin John Sullivan came through the front door.

"Mr. Thomas?"

"Mr. Sullivan?"

The two men shook hands. And John Sullivan handed over Annie's small cloth bundle of belongings.

Then Statia did an odd thing. She took Annie's chin between her strong, wiry fingers and bent the child's head up. Annie was forced to stare right into Statia's eyes — a thing she was not fond of doing. She saw tears there!

Now Statia was putting her other arm around Annie and pulling her close.

"She's trying to *kiss* me," thought Annie, and jerked away. Why would Statia try to kiss her? Why would she cry for her? Annie stared at her cousin. What was going on here?

"Humph!" Statia sniffed. "You might at least be a good girl on the last day."

That was more like it. Annie soaked up the familiar tone, and the thrill of alarm faded.

Cousin John said, "This is Mr. Thomas, Annie. He'll be going with you and Jimmie."

Annie looked up at the man. He was smiling down at her. Annie began to smile back.

Then Statia said, "Give the nice man your hand." That spoiled it. It was just the kind of silly thing Statia always said.

Annie dropped her eyes and skipped past the outstretched hand. She ran down the walk to the carriage. Annie Sullivan would give her hand to no one — least of all to a stranger. She scampered up beside Jimmie.

"Hello, Annie," he said patiently.

This time Annie turned to her brother and smiled. "Oh, Jimmie," she breathed. "Isn't this wonderful?"

Jimmie patted the side of the carriage and smiled back at his big sister. He understood.

So without a backward glance Annie Sullivan rolled off on her one-way journey to somewhere.

Within minutes the carriage had cut through the town of Feeding Hills and left it behind. Soon they were traveling through strange country.

"Look, Annie! Look!" Jimmie could hardly contain himself. "Look at the lake over there, with the swans on it. I wonder why their undersides aren't cold?" And "Look at that house, will you? The red brick one! Four chimneys, Annie. Count. One for each corner."

More often than not, Annie could just cry out

"Where? Where?" Some days Annie could see almost as well as other people. This wasn't going to be one of those days. This was a day when the fog seemed to well up and she saw almost nothing. For the fog was inside her eyes. Annie Sullivan was partially blind.

She strained to see what she could. She listened to Jimmie and imagined the rest.

Too soon the carriage rolled to a stop before the Springfield Railroad Station.

"All out!" Mr. Thomas called cheerily.

The big man laughed and scooped Jimmie out of his seat. Annie hopped down by herself.

Mr. Thomas bought a long strip of tickets.

"All for us?" Jimmie wondered.

"We've a long way to go," Mr. Thomas explained. "Want to hold them?"

"Oh, yes!" Jimmie beamed. His little hand reached up to grab the big one by his side. The man and boy walked hand in hand down the platform. Annie trailed along behind.

The train was great fun at first. But as the day wore on, the fun wore off.

Annie spent too much time looking out the window. Her eyes began to smart. So she closed them.

Then Jimmie began to cry. "It hurts," he wailed.

"What's the matter with him?" Mr. Thomas asked.

Annie had been almost asleep. Now she opened her eyes. "You should see his hip," she answered matter-of-factly. "He's got a bump on it the size of a teacup. They say it's tuberculosis." Annie pronounced the word perfectly. "My mother died of it, you know." Then she closed her eyes again.

Mr. Thomas knew he should feel sorry for these two children. Pity for the boy with his crippled hip. Pity for the girl with her weak eyes. And heaven knows, pity for where they were going.

It was easy enough to summon sad thoughts for the boy. But this girl . . . Mr. Thomas gazed at Annie with distaste. A cold piece.

Annie wouldn't have been hurt if she could have read his mind. She'd have been glad. For who asked him to pity her anyway? Who asked anyone to pity Annie Sullivan?

The sun was beginning to set when the conductor came through the car, "Tewksbury. All out for Tewksbury." The three of them stumbled down the train steps.

At first the station seemed empty. But at the far end a horse and wagon stood waiting. Mr. Thomas led the weary children over to it.

There it stood, an ugly old wagon painted black, and set on high, rusted wheels. Odd, there didn't seem to be any windows. Then Annie saw a tiny air slit that ran around the top of the wagon. The slit was covered with bars. Why? A door was set into the back end — a door that was padlocked shut. Annie knew little about wagons. But something seemed wrong with this one.

Mr. Thomas took out a key and opened the door. "All in," he said.

Now Annie could see two benches inside — one running down each long wall. Annie didn't like it. Somehow it looked nasty in there. So she dug her heels in. Neither child moved.

"What's the matter? You want me to lift you up?" Mr. Thomas made a move for Jimmie. But the boy darted away. He clung to the back of Annie's skirts.

"Now, children . . ." Mr. Thomas began. He was in a hurry to get away. His dinner was cooling on the stove this very minute.

"Now, children, I have to leave you here. But you won't be alone. That's Tim." Mr. Thomas pointed to the driver of the carriage. "He'll be taking you the rest of the way."

A wrinkled little man bobbed his head to Annie and Jimmie. When he smiled, his tobacco-stained teeth showed dark yellow and broken. But somehow it was a kind smile, and Annie felt better.

There seemed to be nothing else to do, so Annie climbed into the wagon. Mr. Thomas quickly lifted

Jimmie up beside her. Then with a quick "Good night," he slammed the door shut behind them.

Mr. Thomas frowned as the wagon rolled away. As a state official, he'd done his job. But it did seem a shame that children so young had to ride in the Black Maria — a wagon used to take drunks, thieves, and murderers to jail. Ah, well. There wasn't money for everything. What the children didn't know wouldn't hurt them. And on this sensible thought Mr. Thomas turned away.

Very little light filtered through the window slit of the wagon. But the cold did. Annie and Jimmie didn't notice it much. They were too busy keeping their seats on the slippery wooden bench as the wagon bumped over the streets of Tewksbury.

After a time the wagon rolled up to a big gate. The gate was quickly swung open, and the carriage rolled to a stop in the inside court. Tim hopped down from his seat and flung the door open. The children tumbled out.

Annie rubbed her eyes. The light was going fast now. But she could still glimpse the gate closing — a big yellow gate closing behind Annie Sullivan!

Tim turned her about and put Jimmie's hand in hers. He said, "Into that building with you now. The nearest one there." Annie stared up at him.

"I'll be right along as soon as I put the horses away," he added more kindly. He'd seen the desperate look in Annie's eyes.

Annie and Jimmie walked up the stone steps. The trip was over. It was February 22, 1876 — Washington's Birthday. And Annie Sullivan had reached the end of her one-way journey to somewhere.

The somewhere now had a name. Officially, the pile of wooden buildings was called the Massachusetts State Infirmary. Some just called it Tewksbury, after the nearby town. Others called it the almshouse. Most people just thought of it as the poorhouse — the state poorhouse at Tewksbury.

The Good Days

ANNIE AND JIMMIE WALKED HESITANTLY through the big front door and into a dimly lit hall. At the far end a man sat busily writing in a ledger. He sang out cheerily, "Come along. Come along, so I can see you. That's good children." From his voice to his lean little shape, the man was altogether like a cricket — a cheerful Irish cricket.

Now he ruffled through his big ledger until he came to a clean page.

"You'd be the Sullivans, brother and sister, am I right?"

Annie and Jimmie nodded. They turned, for they'd heard the driver, Tim, coming through the door behind them. And right now Tim seemed like an old friend.

"Ah, Timothy! There you are," the man behind the desk chirped. "You've already met our Timothy, haven't you?"

Annie and Jimmie nodded once more.

"Well, my name is Mr. Granger. Just a few questions before we assign you to your beds."

Mr. Granger peered at Annie. He picked up his pen. "We'll start with you. Name of Annie Sullivan, hmm?"

"Yes," Annie said.

The man wrote for a moment, then: "What age would you be?"

Mr. Granger waited for her answer. But there was a pause that lengthened into silence.

"Age . . . age," he persisted. "How old are you? When's your birthday?"

When was her birthday?

"I was born on the fourth of July," Annie answered. A lie, as she very well knew — but it was her favorite day, crammed full as it was with fireworks and melting ice cream. Besides, Annie didn't have the faintest idea what her real birth date was.

Mr. Granger wrote down her words.

"July 4. But what year, Annie? What's your age — eight? nine? ten?" She didn't know the answer to this one either. And a handy lie didn't come to mind.

"Turn about then," Mr. Granger ordered. "Like a

top . . . that's a girl. What would you say Tim?" Tim shrugged and looked at his pocket watch.

"Hmmm. Eight, I'd guess." And this went down in the big book too.

Mr. Granger guessed wrong. Annie was small for her age, and slim. But she'd be fully ten next April 14, not two months away.

"That just about finishes the questions for you, Annie. A few to your brother here, and we'll be done."

Mr. Granger turned to Tim. "Ah, it does seem a shame! Children this age in Tewksbury. Why, except for the babies in the foundling ward, they're the only children here."

Mr. Granger took a last look at Annie and Jimmie's page. Name, age, birth date. "Yes," he thought. "all the questions are answered — except the real one: How in God's good name did these children come to be here?"

The explanation began with Annie's parents in Ireland in the years before she was born. It began with their hunger. For almost twenty years the crops had failed in Ireland. Many of the poorer farmers lost their land. Without land, many began to starve. The choice became clear for them: stay and starve, or leave.

In the early 1860's, Alice and Thomas Sullivan left

Ireland with the swelling tide of immigrants that was coming to America. Thomas had been a farmer in Ireland. So he took his wife to the little farming community of Feeding Hills, Massachusetts. He'd heard there was work to be had there. Soon he had a job as a day laborer on a nearby farm.

The Sullivans were a bit lonely in the beginning. But soon more Irishmen came to Feeding Hills. If it still wasn't home for Thomas and Alice, as Ireland was, it wasn't a half bad place to live.

On April 14, 1866, their first baby was born. When the priest came to baptize her, he asked, "What do you name this child?" Alice smiled weakly and whispered, "Joanna." That's what she was baptized. But from the first, everyone called her Annie.

Those were good days for the Sullivans. There was never enough money to put a bit aside, as Alice would have wished. But nobody starved.

The evenings were nicest of all. As soon as Annie was old enough to understand his words, her father began to tell her stories. He would push back his chair after dinner, lift her up onto his lap, and say, "What'll you have tonight?"

Annie's favorite fairy tale was about a will-o'-the-wisp who lived in the marsh. But she was happy with almost anything her father told her. Gaelic fairy tales, songs, poetry — Thomas and Annie shared a deep love of all things Irish.

Many times, before putting her to bed, Thomas would grab Annie and swing her over his head. Around and around the room they would whirl in a wild jig.

"Oh yes, little Annie," her father roared at times like these, "aren't we the lucky ones, we Sullivans? Not a soul on this earth to touch us, for we have the Irish luck!"

"What a Terrible Child!"

THEN THEIR LUCK RAN OUT.

It started with Annie. For Annie was not yet three when her left eye began to itch. There were tiny granules under her lids. The granules were soft at first. But they grew and hardened. And they scratched against her eyes.

Annie rubbed and rubbed, which only made matters worse. The granules wouldn't go away. And the rubbing made them dig all the more deeply into her eyeballs. Annie Sullivan had a sickness in her eyes. And she wasn't getting any better.

The Sullivans were poor, and doctors cost money. So they waited, hoping that time, the poor man's doctor, would cure their Annie's eyes.

They tried home remedies. A neighbor said, "Wash them in geranium water. It's a sure cure." So Alice Sullivan plucked all the leaves off the red geranium plant that grew in the window. She boiled them down in a pan of water. And she poured the bitter brew right into her daughter's eyes. Annie cried for hours with the pain of it. That was the only result. The eyes remained the same.

Finally the Sullivans realized they had to take Annie to a doctor. The doctor peered. He took a tiny knife and scraped off several of the granules. Annie screamed. The doctor snapped, "Make her hold still!"

The doctor was in a fearsome mood. Why did these people always come to him? They nearly never paid. "Sit down, sit down," he barked. The Sullivans perched themselves on the edge of two straight chairs.

"But what is it, Doctor?" Thomas Sullivan leaned forward timidly. "You can help our girl, can't you?"

"I'll give you some salve. Apply it twice a day. It helps with some," was all the doctor would say.

Thomas and Alice Sullivan had a huge faith in doctors. They went away satisfied.

The doctor watched them walk down the street, and he shook his head. There wasn't much hope for that child's eyes.

"Trachoma." It was the word he would not say aloud to the Sullivans. Trachoma — the devil's own disease to cure in the best of homes. Homes where there was sunlight, cleanliness, meat, fresh vegetables, air. Homes where there was money enough for expensive treatments.

The doctor shook his head again. Useless thoughts! If that little girl's parents had money, she wouldn't have picked up the filthy disease in the first place. Trachoma was a slum dweller of a disease. It liked dirt.

That was the first of the bad luck: Annie's eyes. And then there was Alice.

One morning Alice Sullivan put her hand to her throat. It felt sore. The soreness didn't go away, and each day she ran a low fever. Each day she felt more and more tired. When she began to cough, Alice needed no doctor to read her symptoms. The poor knew them well enough. Annie's mother had tuberculosis.

Bad times. It was like dropping a stone into water

and watching the ripples spread and spread. For soon after this Alice turned to her husband and said, "Thomas, we're going to have another baby."

The Sullivans were just finishing their supper when Alice spoke the news. Thomas slowly put down his fork. He swallowed the last bite of food in his mouth. "When?" he asked.

"This winter sometime. Around Christmas, I think."

"Some Christmas present!" Thomas spat out. Then he grabbed his cap off the hook and was gone.

Alice sighed. She couldn't blame him, with the way things were going — her cough, Annie's eyes, and now another baby to feed. The money just wouldn't stretch over things like this.

Jimmie was born in January of 1869. Soon it became clear that something was wrong with him. For he'd inherited more than his mother's Irish eyes. Jimmie Sullivan was born with a tubercular hip.

In the days that followed, Alice grew grim and pale. Later, people told Annie that her mother had been a laughing girl. But Annie's own memories were of her mother sitting so still, white, tired, thin.

Annie still had fun with her father. He continued to sing and dance and tell gay stories — for a time. All her life she remembered the day he knelt beside her and said, "They hurt today, don't they?"

Annie nodded. She knew he meant her eyes.

"Come then, love. It's a nice day for a walk." Thomas held out his hand.

Father and daughter walked five miles to the nearby town of Westfield. Thomas had heard of a new doctor there, one who was said to know about the eyes. So he took Annie to the doctor's office. But after examining her, the doctor could only shake his head.

After they'd left his house, Thomas knelt in the road beside Annie. "Sweetheart, that doctor can't help you. But someday we'll find one who can," he promised.

He swung Annie up onto his shoulder. "When you're a bit older, I'll take you back home to Ireland. You'll wash your eyes with water from the River Shannon. Then they'll stop hurting. River Shannon water," he said the words lovingly, "the best medicine in the world." Annie's eyes glowed. She didn't know how far it was from Feeding Hills to the River Shannon.

Thomas led his daughter through the center of town. And there, in a shop window, was a beautiful white straw hat.

"Ohhhh," sighed Annie, as she pressed her nose to the glass. The hat was banded by a blue ribbon, and blue streamers hung down behind. Thomas looked down at his daughter. He patted her shoulder. Then he walked into the shop.

Annie saw the saleswoman lift the hat from the window. A few minutes later Thomas came out and placed it on Annie's head. It was the first hat she had ever owned. She beamed under the brim of it all the way home. Surely it was the most beautiful hat in the world.

But as time went on Thomas began to change. He didn't know what to do with the multiplying problems and the sadness that gathered inside of him. So he tried to forget his troubles in drink.

More and more often Thomas came home drunk. Alice Sullivan's strength was dwindling. Another baby had been born. Between the wasting disease and the needs of a baby, Alice had no time left for Annie.

And Annie needed time. She was lonely and confused. She felt a great unhappiness growing inside of her, an unhappiness she couldn't understand or control. More and more often it splashed over into angry temper tantrums.

For Annie was already different from her father or mother. Annie Sullivan had worked out her own way of handling the sadness in their lives. She screamed. She yelled. She tore into it with her fists.

Her temper fits weren't pretty, and soon the neighbors took to saying of her, "What a terrible child!"

Once Annie burned herself while tending some

loaves of bread in the oven. It had been pure careless-
ness on her part. But this didn't quiet the rage that was
always there. Annie hit out. Grabbing a poker, she
slammed the loaves onto the floor.

"Oh, Annie, Annie, Annie," was all her mother could
moan, when she saw the ruin of her precious bread.

Another time Mrs. Sullivan told Annie to rock her
sister Mary's cradle.

Annie rocked and fumed. She didn't like this baby
who'd taken the last bit of her mother away. Annie
grew more and more angry. Her hand became more
and more forceful on the cradle, till it tipped the cradle
over and the baby fell out.

That evening her father spanked her. But Annie
didn't cry. She just stuck out her lower lip and got
more angry.

Those tantrums. They grew worse and worse, until
the worst of all . . .

Annie loved to watch her father shave in the morn-
ings. One morning her eyes rested too long on her
father's shaving mug, full to the brim with soap. What
a lovely false beard that gooey soft soap would make.
Annie's hand crept closer and closer. Then her fingers
went into the soap. But this was not one of Thomas'
patient days.

"Get out of there." He slapped her hand away.

The slap did it. The rage boiled over. In a moment Annie had gathered up all the loose small objects she could find and was heaving them at her father's mirror. A thousand fragments of glass fell to the floor. Only the wooden mirror frame was left dangling behind.

Annie was screaming and yelling. Her father didn't shake her. He didn't shout. But he meant what he was saying. Annie heard his words.

"Are you a devil? See what you've done," he whispered. "Brought bad luck to this house. Seven years of bad luck."

Poor Annie. The cause of the Sullivan's troubles lay not in a broken mirror; it lay in poverty and sickness. But on dark nights when she couldn't sleep, Annie remembered her father's bitter words. And for many years she wondered. . . .

Poverty, sickness, poverty, sickness — a circle almost impossible to break through. One year passed, then two, then three. Jimmie became more lame. Annie's eyes grew worse. Mrs. Sullivan sickened. Thomas continued to drink.

Then when it seemed that things couldn't get worse, they did. Through all the painful years, Alice Sullivan had held the family together. But finally the tuberculosis wore her down. One day she was there. The next day she was dead. And the family flew apart.

The Sullivan relatives were forced to come to the rescue. What to do with the three motherless children whose father drank?

A meeting of the clan was called. All the relatives who lived near enough came. And they talked. Aunt Ellen Sullivan volunteered to take both Jimmie and the baby, Mary. But nobody wanted Annie. Her sick eyes. Her temper tantrums.

After a lot of hemming and hawing, the relatives turned to John and Statia Sullivan. John had the money, didn't he? Didn't he own an entire tobacco farm? True, it was small; but it was his own, free and clear.

"You have the most to spare," the argument ran.

"That's pure and simple jealousy!" Statia spat back. But she knew her duty. That afternoon Annie rode home with them.

Statia tried to be kind to this child she didn't want. But Annie fought any control. Freedom was the only valuable thing Annie Sullivan had left, and she fought hard for it. At times she was so rude, so violent, that Statia drew back in fear. Soon there was no more question of discipline. Cousin Statia left Annie strictly alone.

All went well for a while. In the warm months that followed, Annie took to roaming around the farm. From one pasture to another, sitting in an apple tree for hours and dreaming, lying in the mown hay, Annie lazed through her days. She was happy enough when she was away from the house.

"Do you know what I caught Annie doing today?" John Sullivan said to his wife one night. "She was out behind the barn, lying on the grass. She had her hand held up in the air. I watched for fully five minutes, but she never moved at all. It was so quiet. Then a sparrow flew down from a tree. He hovered right over her, just looking . . . then he flew away. Annie held still, and what do you know, that sparrow came back! It lighted on her finger. They just stayed that way, looking at each other like friends . . . strange."

Statia sniffed. "It's no wonder to me. Birds! She's an animal herself. No more upbringing than one of the colts or heifers in the south pasture."

"Still, such a hellion in the house, and so gentle and patient with that bird," John mused.

Fall came. And with it the first days of school. Annie was old enough for school now. And one day, her mouth dry, her voice trembling, she hunted out Cousin Statia.

"Can I go to school this year?"

"Don't be a fool, Annie," Statia snapped. "With those eyes of yours, you can never learn to read and write."

Then it was Christmastime. Almost every day now John or Statia would disappear into the front parlor with a package. For the big front parlor was the place to store Christmas presents. All the children in the house were forbidden to go inside until Christmas morning. Of course Annie went in. Again and again.

One day she saw a beautiful doll, sitting propped up in its own little chair. It had shiny blue eyes and long golden curls. Its china cheeks were painted pink. And it was wrapped in a long, lace-trimmed dress.

Annie couldn't see too well in the gloomy parlor. But even her weak eyes could tell that this was the most beautiful doll in the world.

Time after time Annie slipped in to see the doll. She cradled it in her arms. She rocked it. And sometime during those pre-Christmas visits, she began to feel that the doll was hers.

On Christmas Eve, the whole family trooped into the parlor. John, playing Saint Nicholas, began to hand out the presents. Each child got one. Annie got one. But she put it aside without even looking at it. She had eyes only for the doll. She was waiting to hold it in her arms. Then John picked up the doll and handed it to one of his daughters.

For one frozen moment Annie sat still, unbelieving. Then she exploded. She grabbed the doll by its golden hair and smashed it to the floor. She smashed everything else she could reach before John pinned her arms back. Annie Sullivan destroyed Christmas in that house.

Enough was enough. Another meeting of the clan was called. All the Sullivans met again and talked some more.

They had tried to be kind — truly. But they hadn't wanted these children to begin with.

The exception, Aunt Ellen was quick to point out, was Mary. The baby was real sweet . . . Ellen had grown fond of her. She thought she'd keep her. But Jimmie, now. His hip was growing worse. The medicines cost so much. And Annie! Nobody could manage her.

Before the Sullivans returned to their homes, Annie's and Jimmie's future had been decided. Their one-way journey to Tewksbury had been planned.

The Poorhouse

Mr. Granger shut the big ledger and wiped his
pen carefully on the blotter.

"That's that," he said. "I'm done with the two of you.
Take the boy to the men's ward, will you, Timothy?
I'll see Annie in with the women."

Jimmie caught the meaning of the words a second
before Annie. They were going to be separated! He
threw himself into her arms and began to howl.

Annie's arms closed around her brother. She clutched
him tightly. "No, no!" she cried. "He's my brother!"
And in that moment a new feeling pierced Annie's
heart. The feeling was love. For the first time in her

life, Annie gave over her whole heart to another human being.

Mr. Granger frowned. He scratched his head. "Well, I suppose you can stay together in the women's ward. But he'll have to wear an apron." Mr. Granger had seen the look on Annie's face. He didn't want a scene.

Girl's clothes? When he'd only just been promoted to his first pair of long pants? Jimmie began to howl again.

His sister shushed him. "If that's what we have to do," she whispered. Annie Sullivan was catching on fast.

There were no nurses and almost no medicine in the Massachusetts State Infirmary. Sometimes a town doctor made the rounds through the two long wards — one for men and one for women. But the state did not pay very much, and the doctor didn't come often.

So although some sick were here, this was really no infirmary, no hospital. It was a place for people who had nowhere else to go. Some of the inmates were insane, some drunkards. Most were simply old and poor. They all shared a common bond: they were forgotten people. Nobody on the outside wanted to remember them. Now Annie and Jimmie joined them.

That first evening the Sullivans were given beds in

the women's ward. They were surrounded by sick old ladies, most of whom lay in their beds like phantoms. When they weren't in bed, they sat in rocking chairs, creaking back and forth for hours. The silence of the room was rarely broken with talk.

Annie didn't like most of these old ladies, who seemed more shadowy than alive. Nor their silence and their endless rocking. She was too young to understand defeat.

Most of the old ladies didn't care for the two Sullivans either — children who showed no proper respect for their elders and who made noise at all hours. But in the ward there were two old ladies who became Annie's friends. Annie always felt they were different, that they were still alive. One was a blind woman who held Annie's hand and told her wonderful stories. The other was Maggie Carroll.

Maggie Carroll was desperately crippled with arthritis — so crippled she couldn't even lift herself up in bed. Soon she came to depend on Annie's young strength. When she wanted to turn over or sit up, she'd call "Annie!" Wherever she was, Annie would come. Soon she became Maggie Carroll's hands.

And Maggie became Annie's eyes. For Maggie could read. Annie would hold a book up in front of the old lady and turn the pages when it was time.

Maggie's eyes, Annie's hands. Through the months, they read book after book. And Annie's hunger for the printed page grew.

Annie was happy enough at Tewksbury. She and Jimmie had enough to eat. They each had a bed, pulled close together so that at any time during the night Annie could reach out and touch Jimmie. What if the place was teeming with rats? Jimmie's favorite game was poking at them with long broom straws.

Most important of all, the Sullivans had each other. They weren't mistreated. Nobody in authority was unkind to them. Nobody cared enough to be unkind. Because they left her alone, Annie had nothing to fight against. Her temper lay quiet. Once or twice she started to throw a tantrum, but this always brought an attendant on the run.

"One more peep — *one more* — and your brother goes to the men's ward!" It was a threat that always quieted Annie.

In their first winter months at Tewksbury, it was too cold to go outside. The children had no warm outer-clothes to wear. But the women's ward was large, and at the end there was a small, separate room. Annie and Jimmie took this over as their special playground.

"How can you stand to go in that place?" one old

lady shuddered. Annie only shrugged. She knew what it was. It was the deadhouse. When somebody died in the ward, his bed was wheeled into the little room until the funeral. Annie was as used to the hard facts of death as of life.

Annie loved to poke around. One day she discovered a rat-gnawed pile of magazines in the back of a hall closet.

"Jimmie, look what I found!" She came lugging the old bundle into the ward. They dragged the magazines across the floor and into the deadhouse. Neither Annie nor Jimmie could read a word, but they huddled for hours over the pictures.

Some of the magazines were copies of the *Police Gazette*. These were Jimmie's favorites. But Annie gazed at the beautiful ladies flowing through the pages of *Godey's Lady's Book*. Ladies who wore dresses trimmed with lace. Ladies whose hair hung in well-tended ringlets. Ladies who laughed while rosy children tumbled at their feet.

Holding the magazine close to her weak eyes, Annie devoured the pictures. But pictures weren't always enough. Sometimes her fingers ran over the printed words — back and forth, faster and faster. Then she'd hurl the magazine away and pound her fists on the floor. "I want to read!" the cry escaped. "Now!"

March came. And then April. Then one day it was spring and warm enough to play outside.

But when Annie went outside, she played alone. The pain was greater now in Jimmie's hip. He could only hobble around the ward. He never came outside.

Each day it became more difficult for him to leave his bed. Each morning Annie helped him dress. She helped lift him gently to the floor. She adjusted his crutch under his arm. There! Nothing could be wrong when he could still walk. Annie refused to face the fact that he was growing worse.

But one morning, as Annie was dressing him, Jimmie began to whimper. He twisted out of her arms and fell back on the bed.

The unfriendly old lady in the next bed raised her head now and snarled, "What's the matter with you, little girl? I thought you was taking care of him. Crying all night — kept me awake every blessed minute."

"Shut up, you old hag! It's no business of yours." Annie cried angrily. But she was frightened by the old lady's words.

"Why, you little devil, if I could get my hands on you . . ."

"You'd what?" Annie stood with her arms crooked on her hips.

34

Jimmie loved a good fight. He tried to stand, but couldn't. "It hurts!" he cried. and fell back on the bed, moaning.

Annie gathered him close. "It'll be all right," she promised. "Just stay in bed for today, then it'll be all right." But Jimmie never walked again.

The doctor was called. After he examined the little boy, he drew Annie out into the hall. He put his hand on her shoulder.

"You've got to prepare yourself, child. Your brother's not going to be with us much longer," he said gently.

Annie stared up at him. A coldness swept through her. And then a pain. Annie handled it the only way she knew how. She screamed — she pounded her fists deep into the doctor's soft stomach — she fought back. Some men came running, and Annie was hauled off.

"Enough of that!" the matron scolded. "Or you'll be sent to another ward."

Now? Separate them now? The threat worked once more. Annie went still as a stone.

All through Jimmie's last days, Annie sat by the side of his bed. She told him stories by the hour. She saw that he got enough to eat. When he hurt, she rubbed his back and legs. And she hardly ever slept.

For something warned Annie not to sleep, especially at night. Only a child herself, she felt the special danger that seemed to close in with the dark. She was determined to keep that danger away.

But Annie *was* asleep when they rolled Jimmie away.

When she awoke, it was still dark in the ward. She couldn't see a thing, yet somehow something was wrong. Annie reached out toward Jimmie's bed — and felt the empty air.

A wild fear seized her, so that she began to shake with it. Somehow she climbed out of bed and felt her way in the darkness down the ward. At the deadhouse door she began to shake again. Again she commanded herself to be quiet. Another two steps . . . she put her hand out again — and touched the iron railing of Jimmie's bed.

The whole building was awakened by Annie's screams. Lights were lit, and people came running. Annie was lying on the floor, quiet now. Gentle hands tried to lift her up.

But she misunderstood. Were they trying to separate her from Jimmie this final time? She turned into a tiger — snarling, biting, kicking out. The hands fought with her for a few moments, but then they let her drop back to the floor.

Annie immediately grew quiet again. She lay there for a long time — not moving, not crying. In later years she said it was the worst moment of her entire life. She wished to die more than anything in the world.

Then an old lady hobbled over and tried to get her up. It was an effort, and the woman groaned with it.

The little sound got through to Annie. She opened her eyes. She got up quietly, and helped the old woman back to her bed.

"Come sit beside me, Annie." The woman patted the bed. Then she began to talk in a kind murmur.

"Cry, child. It's the best way. Tears make it easier. Trust me."

Annie didn't seem to hear the words. She sat unblinking, unmoving on the edge of the bed.

"Cry, child. It heals a bit." The woman went on talking softly. All the while she patted Annie with her old, gnarled hand. At last a moan escaped Annie, and the tears came.

"I Want to Go to School!"

AFTER JIMMIE DIED, ANNIE HAD ONLY ONE WISH: to
escape, to put Tewksbury behind her.

Annie knew very well that it was easy to walk out
of the big wooden gates, but she also knew that it wasn't
so easy to stay out. She'd need somewhere to go — a
home, or at least a job. No one wanted Annie out there.

She was too little and too blind to hold down a job for pay.

To stay on the outside, Annie would need help. And within the year it seemed that she might get it. A new priest had been assigned to Tewksbury. Father Barbara was his name. He came every Sunday to hold mass in the women's ward, and on Saturday he came to hear confession.

This was all that was expected of Father Barbara — by his church, by the Tewksbury officials, by the old ladies. But the poorhouse haunted this priest. He took to dropping in for no special reason. He joked a bit and gossiped with the old ladies. He swapped sports stories with the men. All the while he kept his eye on Annie.

And Annie watched the priest. Whenever their eyes met, hers would break away. Silent Annie, still grieving for her brother — it wasn't time to be friends with anyone yet. But even when she looked away quickly, she could see Father Barbara's warm smile.

Each time the priest came, Annie crept closer and closer to that smile. She began to follow him as he went from bed to bed, ward to ward. Months passed. Then suddenly, there they were, walking along together and chatting. Father Barbara was Annie's friend.

Every time the priest left the poorhouse grounds, he gave Annie a special warm smile and a pat on her head. Then there came the day when he gave Annie Sullivan something more: a promise.

They were standing by the yellow gate. Father Barbara looked down at her, frowning. "This is no place for you, Annie!" he burst out. "I'm taking you away from here."

Father Barbara knew that her eyes were very weak now — that she could see almost nothing. He had a friend, a very skillful doctor at the Sisters of Charity Hospital in Lowell, Massachusetts. He planned to take Annie there. If anything could be done for her, thought Father Barbara, this was the man to do it.

After her eyes were taken care of, he would find a house for the child — somewhere away from Tewksbury. But first the eyes.

Almost exactly a year to the day that Annie and Jimmie had rolled up to Tewksbury in the Black Maria, Annie left with Father Barbara. He took her directly to the hospital.

The doctor examined Annie at once. "I think we can help," he told the priest. "Yes, I think we can."

The operation was performed soon after. For many days Annie was forced to lie still with the bandages across her eyes. Then one morning a long procession filed into her room — the doctor, the nursing nuns all clustered behind, and last, Father Barbara. Slowly the doctor snipped off the bandages.

"Open your eyes, Annie," he said gently. And when she obeyed, her heart corkscrewed down through her stomach. But everything was still so blurred! Oh, how blurred. Why, it was worse than before. All Annie could see was light- and dark-gray shadows. The operation was a failure.

"I won't go back to the poorhouse!" Annie cried.

The priest hugged her. The doctor told her there would be another operation. She was not to worry or to lose hope. She mustn't be unhappy.

Unhappy? Annie was jubilant. They were going to keep her here for another operation! She didn't have to go back. Not yet.

For the first time in her life Annie was surrounded by gentle people. People who liked her. People who thought she was bright, who liked to listen to the things she said.

It was a lovely time. But it didn't last long enough. There was another operation. Then another. None of them helped. Finally the doctors decided that they had done all they could for Annie. The hospital was a place for the sick. And Annie wasn't sick — she was blind. She'd have to go. But where?

Father Barbara was no longer there to take care of her. He had been called away to another part of the country. Nobody else wanted her.

"We'll have to send her back," Annie overheard the doctor whisper to a nurse one day. She knew what that meant. She screamed and clung to the doctor with all her strength.

"No, no!" she cried. It almost broke their hearts, but the hospital authorities had no choice. They called for the Black Maria.

Nobody paid much attention to Annie's return. Annie felt as if she were drowning in her misery. But under the pain of coming back to Tewksbury, a determination was growing: she meant to get out.

She made no secret of her resolve, though the old women jeered at her. What made Annie think she was better than anyone else? The old people found it easy to jeer at Annie.

"I don't care what any of you think," Annie cried. "I'm going to leave."

"And my pretty, what'll you do then?"

"I'll go to school!"

This always brought a round of laughter.

Annie's few friends hoped she'd forget this nonsense — forget impossible dreams — for they knew that dreams had a way of breaking your heart. Even kindly

Maggie Carroll, Annie's special friend, said gently, "You're blind, Annie. You can't get along out there. Tewksbury's your home. It's God's will."

"I don't care if I am blind. I'm going to get out of here and I'm going to stay out. I'm going to go to a school — *some* school. And I don't see what God's got to do with it anyway!"

"Shame, Annie!" Maggie was shocked.

But Annie didn't hear. She'd flung herself out of the room.

The months went by, then the years — 1878, 1879, 1880. Annie was still at Tewksbury. She was almost totally blind and no closer to her dream. Sometimes even Annie forgot her determination to escape. But it was a faith that never left for long. She would get out.

One day Annie's old blind friend said, "I don't know whether I should tell you this, Annie. It'll just get your hopes up for nothing, but did you know that there are schools especially for the blind?"

Annie's breath caught. "Where I could learn to read?"

"Yes . . . if you could get in."

Cousin Statia's voice seemed to come out of the past. "Don't be a fool, Annie. With those eyes of yours, you can never learn to read and write."

If her eyes had been poor then, how much worse

they were now! Why, on the record book of Tewksbury she was down as "virtually blind." Annie began to shake with anger.

"It's a trick!" she cried. "You're just being cruel. How can I read with *these*?" Annie banged her hand across her eyes.

The old lady groped about until she found Annie's other hand. She held it for a moment.

"With this, my dear," and she squeezed Annie's hand. "You can learn to read raised letters with your finger tips. With your hands — that's the way for the blind."

Now Annie knew there *was* a place to go. But how to get there? Nobody inside the Tewksbury walls cared to help her. How could she expect help from the outside? How could she communicate with anyone out there? She couldn't write a letter. She was too blind to walk the unfamiliar streets. How?

Annie thought endlessly about this problem, without real hope. Then suddenly, in 1880, the outside world came to Tewksbury.

Most of the time the people of Massachusetts ignored their state poorhouse. But once in a while rumors would circulate about conditions there — rumors so awful that they had to be looked into. This year there was to be such an investigation.

Tewksbury did indeed need to be investigated. In 1875 eighty babies had been born there, and seventy of them had died before the winter was out. The buildings were firetraps. There was never enough medicine to go around in the sick wards. The food was full of weevils. The buildings housed rats so bold they attacked people in broad daylight.

The men who ran Tewksbury weren't cruel. All the state gave them to feed and house and clothe each person there was $1.75 a week. So they just did their job with what they had. Death, disease, dirt, indifference — that's what $1.75 a week bought a person at Tewksbury.

Now the Massachusetts State Board of Charities had heard the rumors, and were coming to investigate. The old people didn't expect much. They'd seen other investigations.

Oh, the men would come. They'd cluck. They'd even be shocked. Then they'd go away talking about reform. The weevils would stay in the flour. The rats would still attack people. Nothing would change.

But Annie expected change. She expected to be discovered. She expected the investigation committee to find her — and send her to school.

One day Maggie Carroll told Annie something she had overheard. "Frank B. Sanborn's his name," she said. "He's the important one. He's the head of the whole group. Talk to him, and you might get out."

Annie remembered the name, and she waited. Finally the day came when word flashed through the wards, "They're here!"

The committee came. The men looked. They asked questions. They sampled the food. They peered into rat holes. They clucked. Annie followed them from building to building, hour after hour, all over Tewksbury. She couldn't see them, but she stumbled after the sound of their voices. All day she tried to work up courage to talk to these important-sounding men.

Then it was all over. The committee was standing by the yellow gate, shaking hands with the director of Tewksbury. In a moment they would be gone — without hearing of her! Her chance would be gone.

Annie didn't know which man was Mr. Frank B. Sanborn. It was too late to matter now. She had no time left.

"It's been very informative," a gray shape was saying.

"We'll send you our findings in a few weeks. Goodbye," another shape added. The gate began to close.

Her last chance was going! Annie hurled herself into the gray mass of men.

"Mr. Sanborn, Mr. Sanborn!" she cried to all of them. "I want to go to school!"

The director of Tewksbury tried to drag her away, but one of the voices stopped him.

"Wait! What's the matter with you, little girl?" said the voice.

"I can't see," Annie managed to stutter. "But I want to go to school. I want to go to the school for the blind."

"How long have you been here?" another voice asked.

"I don't know."

The men asked a few more questions. Then they went away.

That night Annie cried herself to sleep. She'd failed — she was sure of it. But a few days later one of the old women came hobbling into the ward.

"Annie, Annie! They told me to get you. You're to put your clothes together. You're leaving here!"

Mr. Sanborn had enrolled her as a charity pupil in the Perkins Institution for the Blind, not twenty miles away in Boston. Annie Sullivan was going to school!

Her friends quickly stitched together two new dresses — the first she'd had in years. One was blue with black flowers. The other was red. Annie chose to wear the red one on leave-taking day.

Many of the people she'd lived with for four years at Tewksbury followed her down to the gate. Nobody hugged her. Nobody kissed her good-bye. But their advice flew thick and fast.

"Be a good girl."

"Write us a letter as soon as you know how. — Imagine, our Annie!"

"Don't answer back, like you do here."

"Come and visit us sometime."

The driver Tim helped her up into the seat beside him. As the Black Maria rolled away from Tewksbury, Tim flicked his whip back toward the closing yellow gate.

"Stay on this side of it," he said. "Don't ever let anyone bring you back. Never, do you hear? Then you'll be all right."

It was this last piece of advice that Annie remembered best. She remembered it all her life.

So on the third of October, 1880, Annie Sullivan rode away to Perkins Institution — to a new home, to a different kind of life, to a second chance.

A Second Chance

AND SO ANNIE'S SCHOOL DAYS BEGAN. The days that she'd dreamed about for so many years. The reality, however, was nothing like her dreams.

Annie was fully fourteen — a very ignorant fourteen. She couldn't read or write or do sums. She knew nothing about English or geography or history. She was forced to begin at the beginning. Among the babies — or so they seemed to her.

A roomful of six-year-olds, and one big, clumsy, foolish-feeling Annie Sullivan. She felt so miserably out of place. The other girls at school gave her a nickname to show their scorn: Big Annie. And Big Annie they called her at every opportunity.

Annie went through her days bewildered, rebellious, disappointed, always ready for a fight. Each night she went to bed wanting to weep. She pounded her pillow instead, crying, "I hate them! I hate them all!"

Annie had been at school for some months now. She had mastered the art of reading raised print with her finger tips. She could both read and write in the coded dot system of Braille. But Annie couldn't spell. And she didn't want to learn.

What did it matter if she used an E one time, and an A the next? Everyone with any sense knew what she meant. And surely that was the important thing: what she meant. Besides, it took too long to memorize all those words.

Her English teacher tried to explain. "There's a right way and a wrong way of doing everything, Annie. It just takes a little patience. A little discipline." The words meant nothing to Annie.

Then the teacher ran out of patience. She tried another way, but it was a way that hurt.

She took to reading Annie's written composition aloud. At every misspelled word, she would stop. Stop and almost pick the word up off the page in a scornful voice. She'd pronounce it slowly and then spell it out, underlining each incorrect letter carefully.

The other students thought this was great fun. And in the pause that the teacher was careful to supply, they all burst into loud laughter.

Each laugh was like a blow. But Annie just held her breath, and cursed them roundly to herself. She sat through this torment week after week. One day the laughter was especially loud, especially cruel. Annie couldn't take it any more.

"That's right!" she burst out, jumping from her chair. "Laugh! Laugh, you silly things! For that's all you can do to the queen's taste!"

"To the queen's taste" was an expression Annie had picked up at Tewksbury. It meant nothing really, but the teacher thought Annie was talking about her.

"Leave the class!" she told Annie. "Go sit on the stairs. I'll see to you later!"

Annie was boiling with rage, clumsy with it. As she stumbled down the aisle, she knocked against an empty desk. It skittered out of line.

Again the teacher misunderstood. She was sure Annie had done this on purpose. "Come back here at once and straighten that desk!" she ordered. "Then leave the room quietly!"

It was simply too much. Annie kept on going.

"Annie!" the teacher's voice threatened.

Annie continued until she got to the door. Then she whirled about. "I will not sit on those stairs," she announced coldly. "And I will never come back to this class either!" With a bang of the door, she was gone.

Of course the incident couldn't be overlooked. Annie was called down to the office of the director, Mr. Anagnos. He tried to make her see how rude she had been to the teacher. "And that will never do, Annie," he told her.

"But it was her fault," Annie said hotly.

"That's not the point, Annie," Mr. Anagnos replied. "A pupil must be polite to his teacher. Or how can we run a school? You will have to apologize."

Annie refused. Hadn't *she* been the wronged one? And she was demanding no apology.

"That will be enough now, Annie," Mr. Anagnos sighed. "Go to your room. Stay there until you're called, please. Think over everything I've said."

He thought bleakly, as the door closed behind Annie,

"What shall I do? There's really no room for her here. She's too different, too wild. But . . . send her back there?"

There was a knock on the door. In walked one of his best teachers, Miss Mary Moore.

"I've heard about the trouble with Annie," she said crisply. "Will the child apologize?"

"I don't think so," Mr. Anagnos replied.

"Just what I expected," Miss Moore commented. "Too much pride."

Mr. Anagnos looked puzzled.

"What she needs is some personal attention," the teacher said. "She's bright enough. We all know that. It would be a shame to lose her now, when she's come this far. Let me try to work with her."

So Annie was given another chance. Miss Moore set aside some time every week, during which the two studied or talked or walked companionably across the grounds. Soon Annie looked forward eagerly to that hour.

Oh, she'd been distrustful at first — suspicious. And she'd tested this woman thoroughly. She'd say any rude thing that came to mind, and then wait for a reaction. But Miss Moore never seemed to notice. It was as if she hadn't heard.

Soon Annie began to feel quite foolish. It was hard

to be nasty to someone who never got nasty in return. Someone who even seemed to like you, no matter what you said or did.

So Annie stopped being suspicious and gave herself over to the charm of this kind new friend. When she did that, everything began to improve. Her spelling. And her manners, for that was the most important lesson Miss Moore had to teach Annie.

Annie watched and listened, and began to imitate — Miss Moore's soft voice, her gentle ways, her kindly interest in other people. Gradually Annie stopped bristling so easily. She was learning to guard her tongue, too, and trying desperately not to flare out at the other girls when they teased her.

Slowly the manners she imitated became a part of her. As she changed, the other girls began to warm to this new Annie. Then one day Annie woke to a strange feeling inside of her. She was eager for the day to begin — eager to go to class, eager to talk to the others at lunch. The feeling was happiness. For the first time Annie was really happy at Perkins.

Gradually Annie came to be an accepted part of Perkins Institution. Not completely — that would never be possible, because she was a charity pupil. This sometimes caused special problems. For instance, what was to be done with her during the vacation months? The other pupils had homes to go to. The teachers too made their vacation plans. But what about Annie? Even the poorhouse didn't want her as a summer visitor.

The only answer was a job. Annie was old enough for one now. She was blind, of course. But she was clever with her hands. Clever enough to do simple maid's work. Especially if she didn't expect too much pay for her labors.

A job was found for her at Clark's rooming house in the south of Boston. This was a lusty Irish section of town. Annie soon made friends with one of the boarders. They would talk as she cleaned his room each day. He watched as her clumsy movements stirred up the dust. And he winced in sympathy as he saw her eyes growing redder and redder.

"It's a shame," he thought. One day he asked, "Have you been to a doctor about your eyes?"

"To a million," Annie said cheerfully.

"And nothing helped?" he persisted.

"Nothing," Annie replied flatly. "I've been salved and ointmented, bandaged and unbandaged. And I've had six operations."

"How many?"

"Six."

"And not one helped?"

"No — let's talk about something else now."

But the young man had a friend who was a doctor.

"Dr. Bradford is awfully good, Annie," he tried to convince her. "Maybe he can help you."

"Don't bother about me," Annie replied tartly. "It's hopeless. Thanks just the same."

"Why not see him anyway? I'll take you on the streetcar."

"No."

Annie held out for days. Hadn't Father Barbara sounded just like this young man? One of his best friends had been a doctor, too. She wouldn't go through all that hoping again. It was too painful.

The young man refused to give up, and Annie got tired of saying "No." One day he almost dragged her across Boston to meet his friend.

Dr. Bradford was waiting for them at his office. He peered. He scraped. He hummed and hawed, and did all the things that other doctors had done. Annie sat in stony silence, thinking, "I've had this dream before. It's just like the time Father Barbara took me to the hospital in Lowell. The doctor there examined me, just like this, and . . ."

"You've abused your eyes terribly, Miss Sullivan. But I think it's not too late. I think something can be done." The doctor's voice cut into her thoughts.

"I'm putting you in the hospital immediately for an operation," he went on. "Nothing will seem to change with this first operation. But during your next school year, I want you to come back here regularly for treatment. Then next summer, at about this time, I'll operate again. That will be the operation that will turn the trick, if we're lucky!"

"Nonsense!" Annie thought. But she let Dr. Bradford perform the first operation. And during the next winter and spring she dutifully rode back and forth across Boston to his office for treatments.

Then it was her second summer in Boston and time for the next operation. Into the hospital she went. For several days she just lay in bed, resting. The doctor wanted her to be as calm as possible for the operation. He felt that this might have an important effect on the outcome.

"Never fear," Annie thought drearily. "I'm not a bit excited." How seriously everyone was taking this! The doctor came in often to check her pulse and pat her head. Her friend, the young man at the rooming house, brought her a whole pound of chocolate candy. The nurse last night had brought two desserts on her tray. Didn't they know it was all a dream?

Finally the day of the operation arrived. Annie was rolled up to the operating room, and suddenly a nurse was standing over her, holding a wet cloth in her hand.

"What's that?" Annie cried in alarm.

"Nothing bad," the nurse said soothingly. "It's a new anesthetic we're trying out. It's called ether. See? I put it over your nose, and you breathe . . . breathe . . . Smells just like a garden, doesn't it? So nice and sweet . . ."

Annie struggled furiously against the smothering rag across her face. "That's a lie!" she tried to tell the nurse. A garden, indeed! — the stuff was evil-smelling. But somehow the words muddled themselves in her throat. She fell back, sound asleep.

Annie awoke in her bed, with heavy bandages across her eyes. Now the doctor was talking to her. He was telling her to move as little as possible for the next few days. Keep calm. Don't talk. Give the eyes time to heal.

All right, Annie agreed. She'd follow the rules. She'd be a good girl. He'd see in a few days. He'd see when he came to take the bandages off that nothing had happened, nothing had changed.

Finally the moment came. The doctor stood by her bed, gently tugging at the outer tape. Then "scissors!" Annie heard him say. She felt the blades snipping through the gauze pads. The last of the bandages fell away . . .

Annie opened her eyes — and was nearly jolted out of bed. "I can see you!" she hollered. The covers went sky-high as she skittered around the bed. "I can see the window! and *through* it! There's the river! That's a tree out there! I can see you! *I can see!*"

Then Annie held out her hand. And with a shiver, she whispered, " I can see *me*."

A Disgrace to the School

ANNIE'S EYES WERE NOT AS GOOD AS NEW. Everything was blurred, and would remain so all her life. She would be classified as half blind. But to see at all! Such bliss! There was no happier girl in all of Boston than sixteen-year-old Annie Sullivan.

Perkins Institution was a school for the blind. Annie was no longer blind, but she returned to Perkins from the hospital, and nothing was ever said. The rules had been stretched to cover one half-tamed Irish girl who had nowhere else to go.

The teachers soon discovered that Annie's eyes could be very useful, for many of them were blind themselves. So Annie carried messages and ran all kinds of errands for them, like going to the store to select just the right shade of wool for some teacher's knitting.

It was soon discovered that Annie had a real gift with younger children. She was patient with them, understanding, and endlessly imaginative. She was always ready to take them on excursions into Boston. She cheerfully gave up hours of her free time to help put them to bed at night. Soon she became so trusted that she was allowed to teach a class or two.

Happiness was taming the wildness out of Annie. She whirled through her days now. But she was never able to forget those earlier days of blindness, poverty, and loneliness. So she was always especially kind to lonely people. Maybe that was the reason she spent so much time with Laura Bridgman.

Laura was over fifty years old. More than forty of those years she'd lived right here at Perkins. To Laura, it was more than a school. It was her life. Laura Bridgman was deaf, blind, and mute.

She had been born normal, but at twenty-six months scarlet fever had robbed her of eyesight, hearing, sense of smell, and sense of taste. After that, she grew like an animal in darkness and silence. Nobody could communicate with her — until Dr. Samuel Gridley Howe heard of her.

Dr. Howe was a founder and the first director of

Perkins Institution. He was a great teacher. When he heard of Laura Bridgman, he was challenged. Could he reach that barricaded mind?

When Laura was eight years old, Dr. Howe brought her to Perkins. The one avenue of communication left to her was the sense of touch. He would try to reach her mind through her hands, by means of a special manual alphabet.

The manual alphabet was a sign language that had been developed for communication between the deaf. Each letter of the alphabet was shown by a different hand position. Fold the first, second, third, and fourth fingers down into the palm, and tuck the thumb up against the side of the fourth finger — that was the letter A. Reverse the positions to make the letter B — hold all four fingers erect, curve the thumb in on the palm. And so on. Put the letters together in various combinations, and words could be sketched in the air.

But of course Laura couldn't see. Dr. Howe adapted the manual alphabet to her needs. He would wrap her little fingers around his hand as he made the movements. Her sensitive fingers would have to learn the different shapes through blind touch.

Laura was a good mimic. Soon she could not only distinguish the different movements, she could return them accurately into Dr. Howe's waiting hand. But to her they weren't letters — they were merely movements. Now Dr. Howe set about to make Laura understand that these movements had meaning.

He would take an object and let her examine it. Then into her hand he would form the letters of the word that stood for that object.

For a long, long time Laura didn't make the connection. Then one day Dr. Howe put a key into her hand. This was one of the many familiar objects he let her handle every day. Now he formed the manual alphabet letters for key. He wasn't paying too much attention. He'd done this so many times before. But suddenly he felt Laura's hand go rigid in his. He looked at her face and saw a light flash across it. She had made the connection! Her mind had linked the object to its word.

In time, Laura came to know a great many isolated words. But there is more to language than isolated words. Sometimes Laura couldn't string them together correctly. And what of those words that were not the names of objects? What of words like "love," "fury," "friendship," "hate"? It was much harder to get such meanings through to Laura's mind.

Some of them were never even taught. For Dr. Howe was soon satisfied with the size of Laura's finger vocabulary. He was sure it was as far as she could ever go. Then he stopped teaching her any more.

Dr. Howe had freed Laura from her isolation. Not entirely, it was true — but enough so that for many years she was considered a marvel. People traveled from great distances to see her perform her simple tricks at Perkins. But now Dr. Howe was dead, and Laura was growing old. The wonder of her achievement had almost been forgotten.

All the blind students at Perkins were taught to speak through the manual alphabet, so that they could communicate with Laura. But most of them were too busy to bother with an old lady. Laura sat alone in her overtidy room, surrounded by her books, endlessly sewing away.

Annie found it difficult to pass by that room. She felt drawn to the woman who sat so quietly by the window, sewing, sewing, sewing. So she would slip in for a while each day and chatter into Laura's hand. Laura would spell back, slowly, carefully, often weirdly. Annie always pretended to understand what she meant. And in that total silence they formed a friendship of sorts. Meanwhile Annie became very skilled in the use of the manual alphabet.

Annie was always eager to go into Boston. Perkins might be her home now, but she found it a bit small for her tastes. She would haunt Mr. Anagnos' office, hoping he would think of an errand that needed to be run.

Sometimes Mr. Anagnos ran out of errands. Then Annie would have to use the doctor as an excuse. "It's time for a treatment," she would say. And Mr. Anagnos would wave her on.

Annie loved to roam the streets of Boston. Most of the time she was content just to gaze at the sights, or to talk to whomever she could start a conversation with. Once, though, she had somewhere special to go — somewhere very special indeed.

Annie's eyes had been caught by a story in the newspaper. The story told of a hearing going on in the Boston courthouse — another state investigation of Tewksbury. Did she really want to go? But what a silly question. She had to go. So Annie traveled directly across Boston to the courthouse.

Annie had expected to find a crowded courthouse — everyone would be interested in Tewksbury and its problems. But in all of the great hall there were no more than thirty people. Annie tightened her lips. She swept down to the nearly empty first row. And there she sat alone as her past unfolded before her.

The witnesses talked of the gray rats that still came out of their holes in broad daylight. They talked about the spoiled bread and lack of any kind of meat. They told of a fire that had broken out last year. Annie had seen a fire or two in her time at Tewksbury, and she nodded her head, remembering.

Then it was over. They had talked about so many things — the rats, the food, the buildings, the lack of money, and nobody caring. Painfully they had brought Tewksbury to life again for Annie. Strangely, though, they had talked of everything but people — the people in the poorhouse. Somehow she'd been sure she'd hear a word or two about Maggie Carroll, and the old blind woman who told such good stories, and some of the others who'd been kind to her. Or even about those who hadn't. But not a word. Annie left the building in tears.

Perkins was a well-known school in Boston, and Annie had been conspicuous at the hearing in her school uniform. Soon the first whisper of her adventure reached the Institution. In a short time everyone knew that she had gone to the courthouse.

"Do you know the crazy thing Annie's done now?"

"No!"

"Where'd she get the nerve?"

"Well, you know Annie."

"I wouldn't dare."

"A lady wouldn't."

When Mr. Anagnos heard about it, he agreed: a lady wouldn't. He was in a rage.

"Annie, I've put up with a lot of things from you! But this is too much. You've gone into a place no Perkins girl should ever go. You've disgraced the school."

Annie stood there and let his anger wash over her. Soon he would calm down and everything would be all right.

But it wasn't. Mr. Anagnos was deeply troubled.

"Annie," he said, "I'm afraid there's just not room for you at Perkins any more. No . . . I'm afraid this is too much. You're seventeen. I'm going to arrange to have you sent back to Tewksbury. Next year, when you're eighteen, you'll no longer be a state charge. You'll be free to leave there if you like."

Annie said not a word. She stumbled down the corridor to her room and fell on her bed. Tewksbury! Even one more year of it! If she went back, she might never get out again. That was what Mr. Anagnos could not understand. Tim had said, "Don't ever come back . . . don't ever come back . . . don't ever come back. . . ." The words echoed through her mind. It was too much. Exhausted, she fell asleep.

Annie woke to the touch of Mrs. Hopkins, her new housemother. In the instant of waking she remembered, and shrank back. "Oh, not yet!" her mind screamed.

"It's all right, Annie." The motherly woman soothed the frightened girl. "I talked to Mr. Anagnos. I said I'd take full responsibility for you. And I promised that nothing like this would ever happen again." She smiled. "It's all right. You can stay."

A Day to Remember

ANNIE'S NEW HOUSEMOTHER HAD COME TO PERKINS because suddenly she was desperately lonely. A widow for many years, she had lived with her daughter in a little house on Cape Cod. She missed the husband who had died in the early days of their marriage, but there was still her daughter to raise.

Then the girl, who would have been Annie's age, fell ill and died. In her grief, Mrs. Hopkins took to walking the long sandy beaches of the Cape. One day she saw a group of blind children playing in the sand. Who were they? What was wrong with their eyes? She asked a few questions and found out they were

70

Perkins students on a holiday trip. Slowly her interest was aroused. In the fall of 1883, she applied for a job as housemother at the school.

They were as different as day and night, Mrs. Hopkins and Annie Sullivan. Sophia Hopkins, sweet and prim and easily shocked, could never understand Annie's wild bursts of gaiety nor the intensity of her pain. She couldn't understand Annie's temper, her stubbornness, her flights of fancy. But Mrs. Hopkins was looking for a child to love. And Annie was the one she found.

Now Annie had a place to go at vacation time. When summer came, Mrs. Hopkins carted her off to the weathered gray house on Cape Cod. A glorious free time began then for Annie. Full and happy days. In later years, Annie could never remember just how she spent the hours of those wonderful summers. All she knew was that they went too quickly.

Winter, summer — winter, summer. Suddenly Annie was nineteen years old, and this was her last year at Perkins. The year passed in a whirl of studying and tests. Then it was graduation day. There were eight graduates in that class of 1886, and Annie led them all. Annie was to be the class valedictorian of Perkins Institution.

She awoke on graduation morning with her heart hammering against her ribs. After a hasty breakfast, she dashed back to her room. There it was, still hanging in tissue paper in the wardrobe: the most beautiful dress in the world — and hers!

Mrs. Hopkins came bustling into the room. She couldn't help smiling at Annie's radiant face. "It's time to get dressed, Annie," she said. "It'll take quite a while to put up your hair and curl your bangs."

Annie pulled the dress off its hanger and clasped it to her. Thin white muslin with elbow-length sleeves. A long, full skirt just made for the rustle of taffeta petticoats underneath. And three lace ruffles — *three,* mind you — edging the sleeves and hem.

To think that Mrs. Hopkins had made it especially for her, especially for this day! Annie broke into the steps of a faintly remembered jig. She whirled around and around the room, the white dress billowing after her.

"Annie, Annie, you'll collapse!" Mrs Hopkins laughed. "Even before you give your speech. Calm down. Come, I'll help you slip out of your uniform."

Annie whirled over to the older woman, laughing, her nearly black hair tumbling over her shoulders.

"Oh, Mrs. Hopkins, I'm so happy," she cried. "You'll

never know. A day especially for me . . . a dress especially for me . . . and white shoes!" For some reason the white shoes amazed Annie more than all the rest. All through her childhood she felt that white shoes must have been made to be worn only by angels. Mere humans wore plain brown and black shoes. Yet here she was, Annie Sullivan, with white shoes all her own and a white dress too.

"You'll never know how happy I am," she repeated.

"Perhaps not," Mrs. Hopkins commented dryly. It was just this kind of wild gaiety that uneased her tidy being. Then she smiled. She didn't have to understand this child, not this morning. Just dressing her would be job enough.

Through the morning they worked together to transform Annie. First a bath. And on this special day Mrs. Hopkins allowed Annie to sprinkle in a few sweet-smelling crystals. Then into the delicate, lace-edged underclothes that Mrs. Hopkins had worked over for so many evenings. The white silk stockings, and the white kid shoes. A good half-hour with the hairbrush and curling iron, and finally the moment of slipping the dress over Annie's head.

"Now, Annie, I have a surprise for you."

"Another one?" asked Annie, who was fully aware

of just how much Mrs. Hopkins had already given her.

Mrs. Hopkins left the room and a moment later came back carrying the pink sash her own daughter had worn for her high-school graduation, just before her death.

"Oh," said Annie, "I can't."

But Mrs. Hopkins began to wind the sash about the girl's tiny waist. "There!" She stood back. "Annie, you look lovely!"

Annie whirled around to the mirror. "It's me!" she gasped. "It can't be me. I'm gorgeous!"

"It's time to go," Mrs. Hopkins said. And the two of them started on their journey across Boston to Tremont Temple, where the graduation ceremonies were to be held.

Perkins Institution was a unique and very well-known school. It had many important friends and supporters. Many of them were in the audience that morning.

Annie gasped when she saw all those people. She hadn't expected so many strangers. She had thought she would be speaking to a few old friends. Suddenly the speech she had worked at so long and hard fled her mind — every blessed word of it.

The guests of honor were sitting high up on the raised stage at the front of the audience. Annie, as valedictorian, was an especially honored guest. There was an empty chair waiting for her up there. She began to shake as Mrs. Hopkins led her down toward the stage.

"I'm scared," Annie breathed through clenched teeth.

"It'll be all right," Mrs. Hopkins whispered back.

"No, it won't. I've forgotten my speech!"

"It'll come back."

"No, it won't," Annie said desperately.

They had arrived at the stairs to the stage. Suddenly Miss Mary Moore was standing in front of Annie.

"Here," she whispered. "I wanted to give you something too. We're all so proud of you, Annie." And she pinned a corsage of pink rosebuds to Annie's dress. Annie smiled her thanks to her favorite teacher. Then Mr. Anagnos was there too, holding out his arm for Annie to take.

Annie knew this was part of the ceremony. They had rehearsed it. Mr. Anagnos was to lead her up those steps, across the stage, and to the empty seat in the middle of the front row. Now Annie clutched his arm, feeling as if he were dragging her to her death.

There seemed to be no way out. And she still couldn't remember her speech. She would be a total disgrace! Everybody would point. Someone would whisper that she had come to Perkins as a charity student or . . . Oh, no! — the governor of Massachusetts was standing up. This was part of the ceremony too. He'd make a short speech, then turn toward her and say, "And now may I give you our valedictorian, Miss Annie Sullivan."

He'd said it. Annie awoke from her dream with a start. It was time for her to step forward. She was frozen to the chair! Somehow she got to her feet. But now she was trembling so that she couldn't seem to take that first step forward.

The governor waited. Then he stepped back partway to meet her. With an understanding smile, he said again, "Miss Sullivan?" With an effort, Annie managed to walk forward to the podium. Her mind was still a blank.

Suddenly the governor began to clap. The audience, following his example, did the same. Annie had a few extra seconds to collect her wits.

As the clapping died away, Annie squeaked out, "Ladies and gentlemen . . . " Then suddenly it was all right. The speech came back to her. Annie lifted her head and began:

"Now we are going out into the busy world to take

up our share of life's burdens and do our little to make that world better, wiser, and happier. . . ." The words were pouring out in a confident flow.

" . . . Self-culture is a benefit, not only to the individual, but also to mankind. Every man who improves himself is aiding the progress of society, and everyone who stands still is holding it back."

As she closed her address with a simple "Thank you for being with us today," the audience rose to applaud.

The rest of the day passed in a whirl of handshakes and fruit punch and compliments. By late afternoon it was all over and Annie was back in her room, her eyes soft with the freshness of her memories. She didn't want this day to end, but it was time to take off the finery and change back into everyday things.

Annie sat for a long time on the edge of her bed, gently stroking the pink sash around her waist. "I wonder if I'll ever wear it again?" she thought, as she carefully tied and folded it. "And these — I didn't get a spot on them." Annie pulled off the slippers and brushed them with a clean towel before putting them away in their box. Lovingly she fingered each pearl button on her dress as she slowly undid it. Then she sank back on the bed to admire the pretty embroidery on her petticoats.

"Mrs. Hopkins took such pains with all this," she thought. "How kind she is to me. Have I thanked her enough? So much time . . . so much money . . . "

"Money!" Annie came bumping back to reality. She was a graduate of Perkins now. No longer a student. No longer a child to be taken care of. Now she had to earn her own living.

Suddenly Annie felt cold. Quickly she slipped one of her heavy cotton dresses over her head. Not that it helped much. The cold came from the fear inside.

She'd have to think her situation through honestly. The thoughts had been lurking around for months — she couldn't put them off any longer. So then, here she was: twenty years old, unskilled, none too well educated, and half blind. How was that for honesty?

Annie nodded bleakly. It would do. Oh, she could see well enough to read a bit. Well enough to find her way around. She'd be the last to be ungrateful for the miracle of being able to see. But to most of the world she was still half blind.

Yet she had to have a job. She had to earn a living. Or else . . . The one thought that she'd been trying to suppress came bursting through. "I won't go back there! I won't go back!" she cried.

Then the dinner bell rang. All the way down the hall the grim shadow of Tewksbury walked with her. But as she went through the door to the dining hall she forced herself to smile. Her friends would expect her to be filled with happiness. It wouldn't be good manners to disappoint them.

Right after graduation Annie went back to the Cape with Mrs. Hopkins for another summer vacation. But her days were no longer carefree. She was too worried about the future. When fall came, Mrs. Hopkins would return to her job at Perkins, and for the first time in six years there would be no room there for Annie. What was she to do?

Quite a few ideas passed through her head. She thought of getting a job as dishwasher in a big Boston hotel. Surely you didn't need much education for that. And her sense of touch would come in handy. Then she sighed — only men were hired for dishwashing.

Or she might take a job selling books from door to door. That would be fun, Annie tried to tell herself, going from house to house, spreading culture, meeting lovely people. But what about the snarling dogs, the slammed doors, the long walks in the rain, and the days without earning enough money?

By late August Annie had worked herself up to a fever of worry. Then one day came a letter from the director of Perkins:

Dear Annie,
Please read the enclosed letter carefully, and let me know at your earliest convenience whether you would be disposed to consider favorably an offer of a position in the family of Mr. Keller, as governess to his little deaf-mute and blind daughter . . . .
I remain, dear Annie, with kind remembrance to Mrs. Hopkins.

Sincerely, your friend,
M. ANAGNOS

The "No-World"

ON JUNE 27, 1880, HELEN KELLER WAS BORN in the little southern town of Tuscumbia, Alabama. She grew happily and normally. She walked and was learning to talk. Her mind was unfolding day by day. Then in February of 1882, she fell desperately ill with a strange fever. The fever came and went, came and went, and came again. The family doctor feared the child would die of the strain. But Helen was strong, and one day the fever left for good.

The medical man gave a great tired sigh of relief. "She'll be all right now, Kate," he said to Helen's mother. "Children spring back like weeds, you know."

But Helen couldn't spring back. The next morning,

while Kate Keller was dressing the baby, she waved her hand by accident near Helen's eyes. They didn't blink. Strange. Mrs. Keller again waved her fingers close to Helen's eyes. Nothing happened. The child stared straight ahead. Suddenly Kate began to scream. "Helen's blind! She can't see! My little girl's blind!"

For a time Helen lay in her crib, gathering strength after her terrible illness. Then she was well enough to get up. One day, Kate dressed her and sat her down in the middle of the floor. Just then the great bell in the back yard released peal after peal. This was the family signal for the beginning of mealtime.

Helen loved to eat, loved to sit at the dinner table surrounded by her family. At the first sound of the bell, she would drop whatever she was doing and toddle downstairs. Not this time. Now she did nothing. She didn't turn her head. She didn't look up. Nothing.

"Arthur," Kate managed to call, "come here. Quickly."

"What is it?" Captain Keller asked as he came into the room.

"Arthur," Kate whispered, "she doesn't seem to hear the dinner bell."

"Nonsense!" Captain Keller replied. "You can hear that thing in the middle of town."

"I know . . . "

They grabbed a can full of stones, which had been one of Helen's favorite toys, and rattled it against her ear. She didn't respond. They whispered in her ear. They shouted at her. Helen never turned her head. This time Kate didn't scream. She just cuddled Helen close and said in a quiet voice, "She's deaf . . . my baby's stone-deaf."

In a baffled way Helen sensed that something was happening out there. Something she wasn't a part of. And as she grew, that sense of being shut off from the outside world — a world she could touch but couldn't understand — infuriated her.

More and more often she gave way to rages that sprang from her effort to communicate. But no matter how hard she struck against the dark and silent walls that hemmed her in, she could not bring them down.

"You really ought to put that child away," one of Kate's relatives said during a visit. "She's mentally defective, and it's not pleasant to see her about."

"Nonsense!" cut in Captain Keller's cousin Leila. "This child has more sense than the lot of us put together."

Kate sighed. "Bright? Stupid? Does that really matter so much when there's a human being locked up inside, struggling so hard to get out?"

How Helen struggled! Her struggles took the form

of increasingly severe temper tantrums. As she grew bigger, she was fast becoming dangerous.

Helen was blind and deaf. Soon the few words she had learned before her illness withered on her tongue, and soon she was mute too. Her body continued to grow, but her mind was cut off in the dark silence. She seemed more like a phantom than a child — a phantom wandering through a world she could no longer understand. Later, when she was able, she called her world "no-world," and the time she spent there "nothingness."

She didn't know who she was. She didn't know what she wanted. She cried, but didn't know she was sad. She raged, but didn't know she was angry. Her life was bare of love and knowledge. She could neither look forward to tomorrow nor think back on yesterday. People think and wish and remember through language, and Helen's no-world was entirely empty of words.

When Helen was five, a new baby was born to Kate — a little sister named Mildred. Helen understood almost nothing about this sister. All she realized was that Mildred was the keenest competition for the warmth of her mother's arms. So she quickly grew to hate her.

One day Helen reached out for her doll's cradle and found that the baby was inside. Without a moment's hesitation, she heaved over the cradle, throwing the baby to the floor. The family came running at the sound of Mildred's screams. One look at Helen's enraged face was enough to tell them what had happened. Luckily Mildred wasn't hurt. But what about the next time?

"She's growing unmanageable," Captain Keller said sadly. "We'll have to send her away. Next time she may hurt the baby — or even kill her."

"But where?" Kate cried.

Captain Keller just shook his head. Kate knew the answer to her question. There was only one place that would accept a being like Helen: the state insane asylum.

"Let's wait just a little longer," Kate begged. "I've been reading of a place — a place up North, in Boston, called Perkins Institution. Arthur, do you know that back in the 1830's a man named . . . named Howe, that's it! . . . taught a deaf-blind-mute to communicate with a kind of finger language? She was just like Helen . . . Don't you understand, Arthur?" She gripped her husband's arm. "Don't you see? They reached through to a child who was deaf *and* blind!"

"But that was so long ago, Kate," Captain Keller answered. Still, his heart skipped as he sat down to write a letter addressed to the director of Perkins Institution, Boston, Massachusetts.

When Mr. Anagnos received the letter, he shook his head. "How sad," he thought. But there was no one he could spare to send to the Kellers. The school certainly wasn't geared to take on another Laura Bridgman. He'd have to say he couldn't help.

But wait! How about Annie Sullivan? She needed a job. Yes, he'd send this letter on to her. Mr. Anagnos enclosed a note, readdressed the envelope, and dropped it in his letter box.

Poor Annie. She grew more and more unhappy as she read Captain Keller's letter. She didn't want this job. Not a bit of it. Stuck off in a tired old southern town — there was no adventure in that!

Annie paced up and down her room, tapping the letter against her palm. "Who wants to be a teacher?" she thought rebelliously. But what choice did she really have? This was the only offer anyone had ever made her. The next day she sat down to write a letter.

"Dear Captain Keller," she began. "After mature consideration, I have decided to accept your kind offer. ..."

Before Annie would assume the responsibility of teaching a deaf-blind child, she asked permission to return to Perkins to study the detailed records that had been kept on Laura Bridgman.

All through that fall and winter she sat hunched over the notebooks that told the story of Laura's education. She learned a great deal, and none of it raised her spirits. She had always known that it was hard to communicate with a deaf-blind-mute. but she'd had no idea just how hard.

"Dr. Howe was a genius," Annie thought, "or he'd never have been able to do it." There had been others who had tried to help other deaf-blind Lauras, but they had failed. What was she letting herself in for?

One day, in one of the notebooks, Annie read something that chilled her. It was the story of Miss Paddock, one of Laura's early teachers. Miss Paddock had stayed with Laura day and night for three months. She had grown very fond of the child. But one day she had appeared in Dr. Howe's office. "Please take me off this job," she begged. "Laura is a sweet little girl, but I can't bear it. I can no longer endure her terrible silence."

Annie looked up from the book, shaken. She asked herself, "Can *I*?"

The Stranger Arrives

IT WAS THE THIRD OF MARCH, 1887. Two very tired people sat in a buggy by the little country railroad station of Tuscumbia, Alabama. Kate Keller and her nearly grown stepson, James, were waiting for Annie Sullivan.

James broke the silence. "What if she doesn't come at all?"

"She'll come," Mrs. Keller answered confidently. "She wrote and said she would. Mr. Anagnos said she was trustworthy. Anyway, she's only two days late." She sighed. "Maybe something happened to her train, Oh, James, she *has* to come . . . What will become of Helen?"

Just then James caught the faint sound of a distant train. "The 6:30 is coming in," he said. "That'll be the last train for today."

Mrs. Keller found it difficult to breathe. "Please," she prayed. "Please."

Several people climbed out of the train. Only one of them could possibly be the new young governess.

"Looks like a drowned cat, doesn't she?" James commented.

James was right. Annie wasn't looking her best. She'd been wearing the same hot woolen dress for three days and nights. She was red-eyed, low in spirit, and irritated beyond words. It had been such a difficult trip.

She had expected to come winging down here on a fast express. But a stupid Boston ticket agent had sold her tickets for a round-about local that had found its way to every small town between Boston and Tuscumbia.

Well, here she was. She squared her shoulders and

smiled gamely at the young man who advanced toward her.

"Miss Sullivan?" he asked.

Something in his greeting made her smile waver. Annie recognized a condescending tone when she heard it. "I'm not going to like him," she thought.

"Yes," she replied coldly.

"This way, please," he continued in an amused tone. "My stepmother's waiting in the carriage."

When Annie saw Kate Keller, her heart lightened. The two young women smiled at each other.

"Why, she's not much older than I am," Annie thought. "It's going to be all right." It was a friendship formed at first sight.

A few minutes later the Keller carriage turned off the road and onto their own land.

"There it is. That's where we live," Mrs. Keller said, pointing to a roomy white house with green shutters, set back in a beautifully tended garden.

Annie was too excited to notice a mere house. As soon as the carriage stopped, she hopped to the ground. "Where's Helen?" she asked eagerly.

Captain Keller came forward.

"How do you do, Miss Annie," he said. "I'm Helen's father."

"Where is she?" Annie repeated, barely acknowledging his greeting.

"There she is." He pointed to the porch. "She's known all day that something was going on. Days for that matter. She's wild with it."

Annie saw Helen for the first time. The child was standing far back in the shadows of the front porch, half concealed by a climbing ivy vine. Her filthy hands were tearing at the vine, stripping it of its leaves. Her hair lay in a tangled mat on her shoulders. Her blouse was misbuttoned, and her dusty brown shoes were tied with white string.

Helen had felt the carriage roll up, and now she was concentrating, waiting, not knowing which way to jump.

"The child looks so neglected!" was Annie's first thought. Later she understood that on Helen's bad days the family could do nothing with her. If anyone approached, she would fly into a violent rage. This was one of her bad days.

Annie suppressed a feeling of dismay and started up the porch steps. At the first footfall on the boards, Helen wheeled around. She knew someone was coming toward her across the porch. She could feel the vibrations increasing through the soles of her shoes.

Helen expected her mother. For the past several days her mother had been gone so much. Helen had no words to express her need. Now she flung out her arms. And Annie gathered her in.

But this wasn't Mother! Helen struggled and strained like a wild animal to get away from the stranger. Annie, taken by surprise, tightened her arms for a moment. This just made Helen wilder.

"Let her go!" James called out. "She'll hurt you."

Annie's arms flew open. She rocked back on her heels and said, "What happened, Helen? What did I do wrong?"

"She doesn't like to be held, Miss Annie," Mrs. Keller explained. "She never kisses anybody — not since her illness. And she lets nobody kiss or caress her either."

"Except you, sometimes," Captain Keller put in.

James sank down on the porch steps. He looked up at Annie quizzically. "Now do you see what you're in for? You were brought here to teach an animal — governess for an animal!"

"James!" Kate Keller exclaimed. "Stop that!"

"Sir! If that is all you can contribute, you may go inside!" Captain Keller added sternly.

Mrs. Keller noticed that Annie was drooping with exhaustion and said quickly, "Show Miss Sullivan to her room, won't you, Arthur? There's time to talk later."

Annie smiled her thanks to Kate and followed Captain Keller up the stairs.

"Helen wasn't a bit frightened," she mused aloud to his back. "I mean, she was startled, all right. She wanted to get away from me. But I didn't scare her at all. She doesn't know much about fear, does she?"

"No, Miss Annie," Captain Keller answered slowly. "And sometimes that's a problem."

He put Annie's trunk down in the white-ruffled guest room that now belonged to her. "I'll leave you to unpack now," he said graciously. Helen had followed them upstairs and into Annie's room. Now Captain Keller made a motion as if to lead her away.

"No, let her stay," Annie said. "She won't bother me. And it's never too early to get acquainted."

Annie made no direct move to be friendly. She just started to unpack. Helen seemed fascinated with everything this stranger did. Her little hands followed Annie's every motion. After removing the sticky fingers from her open case for the umpteenth time, Annie commented, "Persistent little devil, aren't you?"

Just then Helen's hand met Annie's floppy traveling hat. She seemed to recognize it for what it was, for she picked it up and clumsily tied it under her chin. After touching her way over to the looking glass, she stood

in front of it and cocked her head first to the right and then to the left.

Annie burst out laughing. "Why you little monkey! You must have felt your mother do that! For all the world as though you could see!" Then Annie stopped laughing and looked a little foolish. She had been talking aloud, as if Helen could hear her. It was going to be hard to remember that this child was so completely cut off.

Suddenly Annie's eyes focused sharply on Helen's fingers, now untying the strings of the hat. Two dirty hands, already fluttering about looking for something new to hold their interest.

"You've learned a lot from those hands, haven't you, Helen?" Annie thought. "You've watched your mother get dressed and put on her hat. And a lot else, I'll wager. They're your eyes, aren't they? And you've seen a fair bit with them, too. But I'll tell you this right now, you haven't seen anything yet. Those hands are going to get quite an education in the next few weeks. Those hands are going to set you free!"

The house grew quiet early that night. Annie had fallen into an immediate, exhausted sleep. Helen, as always, dropped off easily into her dreamless state. But in the big master bedroom, Captain Keller tossed and turned. Finally, his movement woke Kate Keller.

"What is it, dear?" she asked.

He was silent for a few moments. Then he said, "It's that girl. She's so young, Kate. Will she do, after all?"

Mrs. Keller smiled and settled back on her pillow. "Go to sleep, Arthur. She'll do."

The Little Tyrant

O N THE DAY BEFORE SHE LEFT BOSTON, the Perkins
   students had given Annie a doll. They had
pooled their money to buy it, and Laura Bridgman
had dressed it in an exquisitely stitched outfit. This
doll was the blind girls' gift to Helen. It lay now in
Annie's trunk, and was one of the first things that
Helen's inquisitive fingers found.

A doll! She recognized its familiar shape. She already had a box stuffed full of dolls in her own room. Helen yanked the toy from the trunk and clutched it close.

"This is as good a starting place as any," Annie decided. She reached for one of Helen's hands, and began to shape the letters D-O-L-L into her palm.

Helen pulled back immediately. But her curiosity was greater than her dislike of being touched, and when Annie picked up her hand again, she allowed it.

D-O-L-L . . . Annie traced the letters over and over again into Helen's hand. Then, by patting the doll's head, she directed the child's puzzled attention to the doll in her arms. Annie repeated the spelling-patting pattern several times while Helen stood transfixed, every bit of her energy focused on those strange movements in her hand.

"Whatever can you two be doing?" Kate Keller came into the room, her arms piled high with laundry. She smiled at Annie. "Tell me just a bit of what you're doing, and I'll be satisfied to keep quiet as a mouse. I promise."

Annie smiled back. Odd, she thought, how quickly she and Kate had been drawn to each other. She was very glad of this friendship, for already she understood that the others in this house — Captain Keller, James, and the captain's other younger son, Simpson — looked upon her as a sort of half-servant. Certainly not as a friend.

Watch, now." Annie picked up Helen's hand, and again she began tracing the letters. "I'm shaping some of the letters of the alphabet into Helen's palm — or shapes that stand for the letters. This is the manual alphabet."

Annie held out her own hands, and her fingers began to flutter through a series of fast movements. "I'm spelling, 'How are you today? It's a pleasant day for a walk, isn't it?' " she explained to Mrs. Keller.

Annie turned toward Helen. "Helen will have to rely on her hands for almost everything — they'll have to be her eyes and her ears.

"This morning I've been tracing the letters D-O-L-L into her palm and getting her to make the letter shapes back. Then I direct her attention quickly to the real doll she's holding in her other arm. I'm trying to connect these things in her mind.

"See! She's going through the motions now. There! She's making the letters D . . . and O . . . and L . . ." Annie stooped down. "And one more L," she murmured, as she helped Helen's fumbling fingers shape the last letter of the word.

Looking up, Annie caught the glimpse of hope on Mrs. Keller's face.

"Of course, it's not the real thing," she hastened to explain. "It's just mimicry — excellent monkey work. Helen can make the symbols of the word "doll" now, but she doesn't have the remotest idea that those particular finger movements stand for all the dolls in the world. I've got to get that across to her. I'll have to repeat and repeat and repeat, over and over again. word, object — word, object. And one day she'll connect them for herself. Won't you, Helen?"

Annie stopped. She wanted to gather just the right words for what she had to say next. "Once Helen has learned this much," she spoke slowly, "the rest won't be easy. But it will be possible."

Annie turned back to Helen. "Come on there. Let's carry this game a bit further!" And with that, Annie reached down and took the doll away from Helen. She wanted Helen to spell "doll" on her fingers, and then she would give back the doll. She wanted to reinforce the connection between word and object.

Helen couldn't know this. All she knew was that the stranger was taking the doll away from her. A weird growl began to grow in the back of her throat. Her face turned red. Her hands locked into fists. In an instant she became a fury. Now she came whirling at Annie.

Annie tossed the doll out of the way and turned

toward the charging child. She grabbed her flailing hands and held on for dear life.

"Give the doll back to her, Miss Annie," Kate Keller begged.

"No," Annie answered. "Then she'll think she can get her way with me any time. And that won't do. If she flies off the handle like this, how can I teach her anything?"

"But it's the only way to quiet her: give her what she wants!"

"No," Annie replied, still struggling with Helen. "There's another way: obedience."

"But Miss Annie, Helen doesn't know anything about obedience. How could we ever teach her to mind?"

"I've got two jobs then," said Annie. "First to gentle her, and then we'll get on with the words."

Helen and Annie struggled on, neither giving an inch. Finally Helen went limp in Annie's arms.

"So," Annie thought, "you give up!"

No such thing! As soon as Annie relaxed her hold, Helen wrenched free and raced from the room. Annie looked after her ruefully. "Well! I wonder who won that one," she thought. "Maybe I went too fast for her. I'll have to be firm, but not too firm. I'll have to move more gradually. Yes — it's as simple as that."

But there was nothing simple about Helen — a fact that Annie was forced to appreciate fully in the next few days.

"Heavens!" she thought after another tussle, "What was I expecting?" And then she began to chuckle. For she knew what she'd been expecting. Another Laura Bridgman, that's what — sweet, pale, and pathetically grateful for deliverance from the silent darkness of her life. Instead here was Helen, this wild thing who fought her at every turn.

"She's badly spoiled," Annie thought. Which was certainly true. Out of their pity, the family had indulged Helen's every whim for five years. Now she was a little tyrant, ruling through her rages.

But there was another reason for the tantrums she continued to throw with Annie: fear. Helen came quickly to fear the stranger. For she soon sensed that Annie was chipping away at the only way of living she had known in her five years. Maybe it wasn't much, that no-world of hers, but it was all she had. And no one could reach in to her to explain that a fuller life was waiting for her now.

So Helen fought for her dark, silent, empty, little life. She fought hard, and without rules. She fought by hiding. She fought by screaming and raging. She fought with her fists. But Helen's favorite way of fighting was with her animal-sharp wits. In her own primitive way, Helen was very cunning.

One day Mrs. Keller handed the child a bundle of towels, indicating through signs that these were to be taken to the stranger. Helen trotted off obediently. Halfway there, she stopped. She laid down her bundle and crept the rest of the way down the hall to Annie's door.

The stranger was in that room. She knew it. Now Helen's hand fingered the door until it came to the keyhole. Ah! The key was in the lock.

Quickly, Helen turned the key, yanked it from the door, and fled with it down the hall. She stopped only for a split second to shove the key under a heavy bureau; then she was gone.

Annie heard that telltale sound. She was over to the door in a flash. Too late. The stout old door was locked. Annie hollered. Kate Keller and the cook, Viney, came running.

"What's happened, Miss Annie?" Kate called out.

"She's locked me in!"

Neither woman standing in the hall outside bothered to ask who. They knew.

"It just doesn't seem she could have done it, with that innocent little face of hers," Viney commented.

"Well, she did," Annie returned dryly from the other

side of the door. "What that child needs is a good spanking. Isn't there another key for the door?"

But there wasn't. Captain Keller had to be sent for, and when he arrived he was not amused.

"We pay her twenty-five dollars a month. You'd think she'd have the sense not to get locked in her room!"

"Yes, Arthur," Mrs. Keller took care to agree. "But meanwhile what do we do? Her room's on the third floor!"

Captain Keller got a ladder from the barn and clambered up to Annie's window. He scooped her into his arms and carried her safely to the ground.

Annie was burning with embarrassment and fury. Here she was, a grown woman, being carried down the side of the house like a bale of cotton! The yard was now crowded with grinning house servants and field hands. It was too much.

Indeed the whole incident was funny, though it would be some time before Annie saw it that way. Even Captain Keller presently began to see the humor in Annie's recent plight. With a chuckle he asked, "Well, what do you think of our Helen now, Miss Annie?"

"I'll tell you one thing I'll never worry about again," Annie replied tartly.

"What's that?"

"Her brain, Captain Keller. When I first came here, I was worried that Helen's illness might have caused some damage to her brain cells. But she's fully equipped. Yes indeed, she's smart enough for ten children — if you like them tricky!"

And with that Annie turned on her heel and fled into the house.

The Battle of the
Breakfast Table

AND SO THE CONFLICT OF WILLS DEEPENED. Sometimes it was funny. More often it was trying. But
Annie remained reasonably full of hope. "Just a little
more time. I'm sure she'll respond," she would tell
herself.

Then came the battle of all battles. The one that couldn't be ignored or laughed away.

It began at the breakfast table. Helen had terrible table manners. She knew full well how to use a knife, fork, and spoon, but she refused to do so. She preferred to use her hands. And not only in her own plate.

Although she would begin each meal in her own place, soon she would slip out of it and begin to roam about the table. Annie watched with fascination as Helen's wriggling nose sorted out the different smells of a meal. She watched with growing horror as Helen's grubby hands dipped and smeared across other people's plates, taking what she wanted, ruining the rest. Yet as long as Helen stayed away from her, Annie said nothing.

Then came the morning that Helen stopped beside Annie's chair. Her nose informed her that sausage lay on the stranger's plate. Helen adored sausage. But this was the stranger, and she hesitated to come closer.

With a little shake of her head, Helen sniffed her way around the table once again. Her nose informed her that nobody else had any sausage left on his plate. Here she was back at that tantalizing smell again. Back at the stranger's place. Was it worth it? One last sniff, and the balance tipped. Out flashed Helen's hand.

Down came Annie's hand. Helen jerked back in surprise, but she couldn't pull free. She was pinned to the table. Slowly Annie began peeling the little fingers away from her sausage.

"Just what do you think you're doing, Miss Sullivan?" Captain Keller asked.

"I'm taking my sausage back," Annie replied coldly.

"Miss Sullivan, that is an afflicted child," Captain Keller pointed out, as if talking to a simpleton. "We have always made allowances for that."

Annie took a long breath and tried to contain her rising temper. If only the Kellers would stop interfering!

"Captain Keller, I know Helen is desperate and frustrated and handicapped. But she's also terribly spoiled. And that doesn't have to go on!"

Captain Keller half rose out of his chair. "No child of mine is going to be deprived of her food in my house!" He was furious.

So was Annie. "And no child in my care is going to help herself to food from my plate!" she shot back.

James choked back a laugh, and gazed at Annie with a new appreciation in his eyes.

"Do you have something to say, James?" Captain Keller asked ominously.

"Nothing, sir," the young man answered hastily.

"Now, to make myself completely clear, Miss Sullivan," Captain Keller went on. "I will repeat once more: as long as I am at the table, Helen will not be interfered with."

"Then perhaps it would be easier if you all left the room," Annie snapped.

That did it. "Miss Sullivan, I am sorry to tell you . . ." But before he could finish his threatening sentence, Kate Keller had thrown down her napkin and was at his side, urgently whispering in his ear.

"Come, dear. You promised that Miss Sullivan could have a free hand with Helen. You know you did. I understand what she's doing. Truly I do."

Annie winced at her next words. "It's not as cruel as it looks. Really it isn't. It's for Helen's good. Come, let's do as she asks. Let's go outside onto the porch. I'll explain it all. Come, dear. Come, James." Gently Kate Keller ushered the family out.

So they were alone, phantom and the stranger — just the two of them.

Annie got up and locked the dining-room door. Pocketing the key, she side-stepped Helen, who was rolling and raging on the floor, and returned to her seat.

"This is going to choke me!" thought Annie, as she picked up her fork. But she wanted to impress on Helen that life would go on as usual, tantrum or no tantrum. So now she began to chew slowly on her cold breakfast.

That next half-hour dragged for both of them. Annie

went through the motions of eating. Helen continued to pound away on the floor. Finally she got bored. Where was everybody? Why were they ignoring her? Curiosity slowly got the better of rage, and as suddenly as it had begun, the tantrum stopped.

Now Helen picked herself up and wandered over to see what the stranger was doing. So the stranger was eating, was she? One hand patted Annie's arm, as the other hand crept out toward her plate. Annie pushed the hand away. But Helen was hungry and determined. Her hand came forward again — this time with more speed. And again Annie pushed it away — this time a little more roughly than before.

Now Helen exploded into a small rage. She pinched Annie cruelly on the arm. Without a moment's hesitation, Annie slapped Helen's hand as hard as she could.

Helen jerked back. That had hurt! But it was something she could understand. She reached forward and pinched Annie again. And Annie slapped back. Pinch, slap — pinch, slap. Each time Helen pinched, a stinging slap would come sailing out of the dark.

Suddenly Helen veered off and made a quick tour of the table. All the seats were empty! She dashed across the room. She yanked at the door, but it wouldn't open. Her fingers sought the key, but the keyhole was empty and the door was locked. For the first time she seemed to realize that she was alone with the stranger. Locked in with her enemy, and all the understanding arms gone!

"Oh, Helen, I won't hurt you," Annie murmured, as she watched Helen flatten herself against the door. With strange animal movements, the child began to inch around the walls, keeping as much distance as she could between herself and the stranger.

Annie sighed and rested her head in her hands. Perhaps she'd better unlock the door . . . perhaps it was too much to expect. But no! "I'll see this through, no matter what," Annie decided, and she picked up her fork again.

As time passed, Helen got hungrier and hungrier. The stranger was still at the table. Dare she go close? More time passed, and the hunger grew stronger. Finally, making sure not to touch the stranger on the way, Helen returned to her seat and began to eat her oatmeal — with her fingers.

"Oh no!" Annie sighed. "I thought we'd won. You know what you're doing, Helen. I know you do. You're just defying me again. And I can't let you get away with it. Not this time." So Annie got up and handed Helen her spoon.

Helen held the spoon for a moment. Then she flung it to the floor. Forcing Helen out of her chair and down to the floor, Annie made her pick up the spoon. And then she plunked Helen back into her seat. She held her hand, and with steely strength forced the child to scoop up some cereal and carry it into her mouth.

One bite. Then two. Good. Annie began to relax her hold. But too soon. For in that instant Helen took aim and hurled the spoon at Annie.

Annie ducked. The spoon clattered to the floor. And the whole process began again. Helen screamed and kicked. Annie held on firmly, and just as firmly she forced Helen through the motions of polite eating. This time, when Annie finally relaxed her hold, Helen kept right on eating. How hungry she was. And oh so tired! She finished her breakfast without further battle.

"It's almost over, it's almost over!" Annie sang to herself, as she watched the food disappear. But not quite. For as soon as Helen scraped the last of the food from her plate, she yanked the napkin off her neck and threw it to the floor.

"My, you do like to throw things, don't you?" Annie whispered. "Well, throw away. You're stubborn, but I'm just as stubborn. You're strong, but I'm a little stronger — thank God! You hate it now, but that little edge of strength will save us. So I can't let you go just yet. I can't let you leave before you fold that napkin. Come on . . ."

And so they fought one more battle that morning —

over a properly folded napkin. It lasted another full hour. Helen fought like one possessed, and so did Annie. At last it was over. A tiny shiver shook Helen's body, and she went limp.

Now her fingers followed Annie's promptings — fold, fold again, and fold once more. There. A properly folded napkin. With a sigh, Helen sank back in her chair. It was all over.

"And so is the morning," Annie realized with dismay, as she unlocked the door and led Helen out into the garden. "We spent the whole morning in that dining room!" For the sun was overhead, and Annie could hear the sounds of lunch being prepared in the back kitchen.

"But not for me," she breathed. "I may never be able to eat again." She looked down at Helen sitting listlessly on a bench. "And I bet poor Helen won't either."

Annie left Helen in the garden and walked back toward the house. Wearily, she climbed the steps to her room. With a great sigh of relief, she loosened her skirts and flopped down across the bed. For a few seconds everything was quiet. Then the tears came pouring out.

Alone with *Her*

KATE KELLER WAS SITTING on the vine-shaded side
porch, with a basketful of socks. But it was hard
to concentrate on darning. Her thoughts were too
troubling.

She had been severely shaken by the wild sounds
coming through the dining-room door all morning.
Had she been wrong about Annie Sullivan? Was she
simply allowing poor Helen to be senselessly tortured?

That's what Arthur had said. The sounds in there
had driven him straight out of the house. He hadn't
returned yet, but she knew what he'd say when he did:
"Send her packing!"

And yet . . . James took just the opposite tack.

115

Strange, too, since in the beginning he had been so skeptical of the new teacher. Now he was saying that this was the best thing that had ever happened to Helen . . . that it would be the saving of her — if the family allowed it.

What did *she* think?

"I don't know," Kate thought in despair, as she pricked her finger with the darning needle for what seemed like the hundredth time that afternoon. Just as she put the basket aside, Annie appeared at the door.

"May I come out, Miss Kate? I've been looking for you everywhere."

"Yes, do," Kate replied. "I've been wanting to talk to you too."

Annie was too impatient to listen. The words poured out. "Miss Kate, I've been upstairs in my room for hours, thinking. There's no other way. I tried and tried to think of another — but there isn't one. I've got to take Helen away from here. Now. I've got to separate her from the family, or I'm going to fail."

"What are you saying?" gasped Helen's mother.

Annie struggled frantically to find the right words — soft words — for what she had to say. Finally she used the only words there were. Words of truth.

"Miss Kate, before I came here I studied Laura Bridgman's records. I felt ready to teach Helen to communicate. When I got here, I soon realized that teaching Helen could only come second. She's completely wild! And that's my first job: to tame that wildness — the wildness nobody else has controlled in five years!"

Kate's lips began to move, to protest. But Annie hastened on.

"I know you did it out of pity. That's why you gave in at every turn. But Miss Kate — I'm sorry — it was a mistake. Those five years of pity have made her into a little tin god. She will or she won't, and that's the end of it. Please try to understand. That willfulness of hers is a kind of not listening. And I've got to have her listening to me, or how can I teach her anything?

"A few more sessions like this morning's, and one of two things is bound to happen. Either she'll go completely wild, like some maverick animal, and never let me near her again, or she'll learn to mind . . . Oh, yes. But the wrong way — not through understanding and warmth, but because I've broken her will. Why then she'll be of no more value to herself than one of Captain Keller's horses!"

Kate winced. "But what can we do?" she cried out. "You make it sound as if there's so little hope!"

"Oh yes, there is hope — some." Annie spoke softly

now, persuasively. "But not if we stay here. If we stay here, she'll just keep on turning to you and fighting me. Soon she'll start hating me. Then it'll be all over. I'll have to pack up and go home.

"But if I can get her away somewhere, where we're alone. Just for a little while, Miss Kate. Just till I make some kind of calm contact with her. Just till she learns to depend on me. Please . . ." Annie leaned forward in her chair, frankly begging now.

Mrs. Keller looked dubious.

"It's our only hope, Miss Kate."

Finally Kate nodded. "All right." Then she added grimly, "Captain Keller won't like this. He'll hate it, in fact. But I'll talk him around."

"Thank you, Miss Kate! You'll see, it will be all right." Annie's spirits soared. "Where can we go?"

"Well . . . there's a little garden house near here. That might do. It has one room, but it's quite lovely."

"It sounds perfect! That's all we need, Helen and I — one room to be together."

As Kate had said, Captain Keller wasn't happy about the idea. He'd come home, in fact, raring to fire the Yankee snippet. Now this!

Kate kept repeating Annie's words: "It's our only hope. It's our only hope." She reminded him that there was only one other place for Helen to go . . . Surely the garden house was not as bad as that. At last, reluctantly, Captain Keller agreed.

"But only for two weeks! Do you hear me, Kate? Two weeks — that's all the time I'll give her. And we've got to be able to see Helen every day."

"Two weeks! Not long enough," Annie thought. But she wouldn't dwell on it. Two weeks would have to do. Captain Keller had been firm about that.

Annie was equally firm. The Kellers could see Helen every day, but the child must never know they were near. They could watch her to their hearts' content through the window of the garden house, but they could come no closer.

The next day the experiment began. At first it seemed that nothing would be accomplished. Helen fought Annie at every turn, to the point of exhaustion. Then she huddled for a while, gaining strength for another bout. After three or four days the pattern began to change. The tantrums were still violent, but they became fewer and fewer. Helen's attention span was lengthening, too. She was learning to mimic more and more words each day. One day there were no temper squalls at all. And then there came the moment when Annie reached out to touch Helen, and Helen didn't shrink away. The experiment was beginning to work!

Captain Keller saw this too. One morning he stood outside the window, watching his daughter string beads onto a length of thread. First a big rough one, then two small smooth ones, then one with three sharp corners. Over and over Helen repeated the pattern. Her interest never flagged. Her fingers never made a mistake.

"How quiet she is," Captain Keller murmured. Had he been wrong all the while about this Yankee girl? Did she really know what she was doing?

The little savage had learned to obey. It was a great step forward. But Annie was only half satisfied. All her attention now focused on the second goal: to reunite Helen with the world outside.

Hour after hour, Annie sat beside Helen and spelled words into her hand. Hour after hour Helen traced the shapes back into Annie's waiting palm. How Helen concentrated! She could spell back twenty-one words — eighteen nouns and three verbs: doll, mug, pin, key, dog, hat, cup, box, water, milk, candy, eye, finger, toe, head, cake, baby, mother, sit, stand, walk. But though she learned the words faster and faster, she still did not understand that they had meaning.

"Hurry up, Helen. Hurry!" Annie begged over and

over. For the two weeks' time in the garden house was running out. How much she wished to lead a different Helen out of here — a Helen who grasped the meaning of words.

The last afternoon came too soon. "Miss Annie . . ." Captain Keller came walking into the room. "It's time to go home. If we hurry, we'll be in good time for supper."

Helen had been playing across the room by the fireplace. Suddenly she felt the strange vibrations. She raised her head and sniffed the air. That was her father's smell! With a cry of joy, she flung herself across the room and into his arms.

Father and daughter hugged each other hard. Then Helen raised her head and began to sniff again. Another smell? She recognized this one, too. Her father had brought his hunting dog with him. Helen felt her way around the room until her hand met up with the furry coat of her old friend, Belle.

Annie turned toward Captain Keller again. "Just give us a few more days, sir," she begged. "You can see how happy she is. And oh, she's learning so fast. You wouldn't believe it. Just a few more days of concentration, and I'm sure a breakthrough will come."

"Well . . . " Captain Keller wavered.

"He's going to agree!" Annie thought jubilantly.

Just then Captain Keller asked in a puzzled voice, "What's she doing now, Miss Annie?"

Helen was sitting cross-legged on the floor, holding one of Belle's paws in her hand. With her other hand she was pushing the dog's claws back and forth. Then she dropped Belle's paw and began to shape some letters with her hand.

Annie began to laugh. "Why, she's trying to teach Belle how to spell."

They shared a laugh. Then Captain Keller grew sober. "It's all well and good," he said heavily. "But we know dogs can't learn English. Can Helen?" And he made them pack up and come back to the house.

W-A-T-E-R

ONE MORNING SOON AFTER THEIR RETURN to the big
house, Helen and Annie were sitting side by side
on the bedroom floor. Annie had Helen's hand im-
prisoned in hers — spelling, spelling, spelling more
shapes into it.

M-U-G she spelled. Then she guided Helen's

hand over her own breakfast mug. M-U-G. Helen shaped back obediently. M-U-G . . . M-U-G. But her heart wasn't in it. Not today. This weary game of shapes was fast losing interest for her.

The smells of spring were pouring in through the open window. She tugged at Annie's sleeve. Clearly she was asking to go outside.

"Not yet, Helen," Annie spelled. "Just a few more minutes. Then the lesson'll be over and we can go outside."

Helen felt the strange shapes of Annie's speech being formed in her palm. But she still didn't know that the shapes were words, that they held meaning. It was this that was building up her frustration now. For there was a dim awareness inside of her: the stranger wanted something from her — something she simply didn't know how to give. And besides, those smells! The outdoors was calling too strongly. Helen jerked again at Annie's arm. Much harder this time.

"Oh, no!" Annie exclaimed, as she saw the telltale signs of rising temper. "I'm simply not equipped to handle it this early in the morning! Come on!"

Annie led Helen outside. As soon as Helen felt the sun on her face, she began to skip and dance. She was getting her own way! The lesson must be over!

The two of them rambled through the middle of the

garden, Annie letting Helen stop whenever she wanted to smell the flowers or roll in the grass. It seemed for all the world as if they were out for a casual stroll. But stubborn Annie still intended to salvage something from the morning.

She led Helen down to the old well house that stood at the foot of the garden. Helen loved to play in its cool dampness, so now she scurried cheerfully inside. Annie took a deep breath and followed.

She began to bang the pump handle up and down, and soon a stream of water poured from its lip. She grabbed Helen's hand and stuck it under the icy flow, and in the same instant began to spell W-A-T-E-R into the wet palm.

Helen went rigid and pulled wildly toward freedom. But Annie held on. W-A-T-E-R . . . W-A-T-E-R . . . W-A-T-E-R — she drummed the word faster and faster into Helen's hand.

Suddenly Helen stopped struggling. Or breathing. Or doing anything except concentrating on the shapes in her palm. W-A-T-E-R . . . she felt the word burn down through her hand and into her brain. W-A-T-E-R . . . a light flooded across her face.

W-A-T- . . . she began to spell the word back to Annie. And with each movement of her own fingers, the namelessness retreated. She understood! These movements stood for the cold liquid that was pouring over her hand! They *always* stood for that, and nothing else! She understood!

Life came rushing in on Helen. Now she dropped to the ground and struck it with her fist. Laughing, crying, Annie knelt down and hugged her. But Helen had no time for this! She pushed Annie back, and again struck the ground. "Name it!" she was demanding. And Annie did.

Helen paused for a moment to absorb the shapes. Then she wheeled round and hit the pump. P-U-M-P . . . Annie fluttered off on her fingers. Helen stood on one leg, concentrating on this, her third word in as many minutes. With a short nod she added it to her growing pile. Then, with ever-increasing speed, she whirled around and around the well house, demanding the names of everything she touched.

After six or seven more words, she stopped. She cocked her head, and it was clear to Annie that she was puzzled. There was something she wanted to know. Helen frowned as if she were heading into another rage. But she wasn't. It was the effort of shaping thought without words. Now she took her fist and banged herself across the top of the head.

Annie burst out laughing. "So that's it!" she exclaimed. "Come, rascal, give me your hand."

H-E-L-E-N, she spelled slowly into it.

It didn't seem possible, but the light grew brighter in Helen's eyes. She stood very still for a moment, with her face raised toward Annie. She had a name.

Now she took Annie's hand and very gently patted her on the arm. Annie thought she was saying "Thank you." But Helen wanted something more. She patted Annie's arm again.

"Oh," said Annie, as she knelt beside Helen and spelled T-E-A-C-H-E-R into her hand. Now the two of them had names.

So it happened that a few minutes later two entirely new people walked out of the well house. Teacher had come to take the stranger's place. Phantom was gone too; instead there was Helen.

Full of the joy of understanding, Helen continued to reach out for Teacher, begging for new words. Before bedtime that evening, Helen had learned to spell more than thirty words. More words in one day than she'd learned in all the five weeks since Annie had come — and she knew their meanings too!

Now her fingers were trembling with exhaustion. She fumbled the shapes, and her eyelids drooped. "Enough's enough," Annie thought, as she tucked her in the bed they now shared.

Helen settled down happily, but Annie had to laugh

as she watched her hands. "There'll be time for that tomorrow, Helen!" she murmured. "There'll be a lot of tomorrows now." And she reached down to quiet the fingers which were still moving against the sheets.

Annie stood beside the bed, realizing for the first time that day just how tired she was. Quickly she slid into her nightgown and climbed in beside Helen. No face washing or teeth scrubbing tonight.

"Ah, the end of a wonderful day," she thought, and wriggled her toes against the cool sheets.

But the day wasn't quite over. For Helen was still awake, and now she came stealing over to Annie's side of the bed. After dropping a damp kiss onto Annie's cheek, she snuggled down in the crook of her arm and fell asleep.

Annie lay there, holding the sleeping child. Then she bent down and kissed Helen back.

Words — and More Words

Now Annie flooded Helen's hand with words. And Helen learned with astonishing speed. She didn't know she was learning. Helen was much too busy to know anything. She had five years of word hunger to satisfy. And satisfy it she did.

By the end of April, Helen knew more than one hundred words. By the middle of May, almost four hundred words. Even more important, many common idioms were locked in her fingers.

It was time to teach her to read. Annie got out her equipment — a pile of cardboard slips with one simple word printed on each. Each word was raised from its cardboard background so that Helen could read it with her finger tips.

Annie selected a card at random. "B-O-X will do," she thought. She placed the card on top of a real box. She directed Helen's fingers over the printing on the card, then moved her hand down to investigate the box underneath. Word, object — word, object. She carried Helen's hand back and forth, but Helen did not seem to make the connection between the label name and the real box.

Patiently, Annie tried other objects and other words. Somehow she wasn't getting through. No matter how hard Helen tried — and she almost burst her heart with trying — she couldn't turn the puzzle into sense.

Annie changed her tactics. She used an alphabet sheet made especially for the blind. She put a finger of Helen's right hand on the raised letter A. And at that exact moment she sketched the letter A into Helen's free left palm. Helen frowned. Understanding was coming through her left hand. But what was happening under her right?

Slowly she moved her own finger to the next raised letter. Annie quickly made the shape of B in Helen's palm. Now with ever-increasing speed, Helen moved on to C and D and then E, Annie keeping up all the while with her letters.

Suddenly — perhaps between the E and F — understanding came. Helen began to smile. "So," she seemed to be saying, "there's a bigger world for me."

Helen mastered the twenty-six letters of the alphabet quickly. Before the next day was over she had moved on to words. And for a while she was content with this. She studied her word cards, and spent happy hours searching for isolated words she knew in the raised-print primer that Annie now gave her.

Annie was glad to let her rest at this point. The weather had turned brutally hot, and surely Helen needed to rest that overactive brain of hers. But Helen was hard to slow down, as Annie soon found out.

"Here," she spelled one morning, handing Helen some word cards. "Teacher has to go downstairs this morning and help Mother. Helen must stay here and study by herself. Yes?"

Helen frowned, but nodded "Yes." Annie left the room.

Helen fingered the cards for a moment. Then she flung them aside. What did she want with those old cards? What more could they offer her? She already knew all the words on them.

Helen sighed. She cupped her chin in her hand. When would Teacher come back? Should she follow her downstairs? No, Teacher had said to stay here. Helen sighed again.

Suddenly her eyes narrowed. She pulled the cards back toward her again — eagerly now. And she began to finger her way through them. Ah! Here was one she wanted . . . and this would do too. Now where was it? Here it was! And this one too. There — that was enough.

Helen hopped down from her chair. She felt her way over to the wardrobe and opened the door. Quickly she ran her fingers over the cards she held in her hand. Then she stooped down and spaced three of them out on the floor of the wardrobe. The fourth card she clutched in her hand.

She got into the wardrobe and stood there for a moment. Nothing happened. So she ran out to the bedroom door, cocked her head, and held herself tense, trying to feel the vibrations out in the hall. Nothing vibrated. Teacher must still be downstairs.

Helen stood quietly for a moment, but not for long. She was too excited. Now she tore back to the wardrobe again. She brushed her fingers over the cards. Yes, they were still in the right order. She skipped back to the bedroom door again. Everything was still quiet in the hall.

Back and forth, back and forth across the room went Helen. Would Teacher never come? Then Helen felt the first vibrations on the stairs. Was it Teacher? Now the vibrations had grown into footsteps in the hall. Yes, it was Teacher!

Helen hugged herself with delight. She could imagine Teacher looking for her in the empty room. Where was Helen? Where could that child have gone? Would she search for her? Surely she would . . .

And she did. Annie had seen the wardrobe door swing as she came into the room. So Helen was playing a trick, was she? Annie smiled and went over to the wardrobe. Ever so gently she pulled the door open. And there was Helen.

Suddenly the fond smile left Annie's face. Tears sprang to her eyes. "Oh my darling girl," she gasped. For a moment she was too overwhelmed to move. Helen was standing before her in the wardrobe, proudly holding up a card that spelled G-I-R-L. Beside her on the floor were three more cards. They spelled I-S and I-N and W-A-R-D-R-O-B-E. It was Helen Keller's first sentence, and she had done it by herself.

Annie knelt down beside Helen and softly spelled into her hand, "Helen makes Teacher very happy."

Lessons from Life

THE LITTLE GIRL WHO'D BEEN LOCKED AWAY in dark silence would never be quite so lonely again. She would never see the world outside. She would never hear it. But she was learning to communicate. And in so many ways!

She could talk with her fingers and listen with her palm. She was fast learning to read the raised print letters. Soon Annie would teach her how to make the shapes of those letters with her own pencil. Then she would be able to put her thoughts down on paper. She would be writing. Next would come the mastery of Braille, that exciting tool for both reading and writing.

Helen and Teacher didn't spend all their time indoors hunched over books and papers and pens. Annie knew that there were important lessons to be found in the physical world around them — lessons from life.

A baby chick damply pecking its way out of a shell; a butterfly frantically beating its wings against Helen's cupped palm; five puppies dashing and tumbling across the barn floor; the special piercing vibration that could only be a cat's mew; the strain of a fishing pole as a catfish nibbled on the end of the line. Annie went out and stuffed Helen's mind with life.

Each morning after breakfast the two of them would set out from the house. They had a destination: Keller's Landing, an unused loading wharf on the Tennessee River. It was only two miles away, yet they were never sure of covering those two miles before it was time to turn back for lunch. For there were lessons at every step. All it needed was a question from Helen, and Annie was off.

Squelching her own nervousness, Annie would plunge her hand under a cabbage plant and come up with a wriggling frog. Then Helen would hold it in her hand.

With her fingers, Helen felt a cricket's back legs vibrate into the sound that she couldn't hear with her ears.

Helen fingered the soft fibers of a bursting cotton boll, as Annie spelled out what cotton could be made into, what it meant economically to the South, the part it had played in the recent Civil War.

Helen memorized the shapes of wildflowers as Annie described the colors she'd always have to take on faith. There were some things they could share in equally. The delicious smell of wild strawberries ripening in the sun — and the taste of them too, as they stuffed their mouths with their goodness. The feel of the grass drying in the sun, or the smoothness of a lightning bug.

Usually they made it down to Keller's Landing sometime in the morning. It was there, on the banks of the Tennessee River, that Helen first learned geography.

Teacher knelt in the mud, building it up into peaks here, digging it out there. Now several big, odd-shaped holes appeared, very deep. And a long, flat plain, and some ridges. Then Annie leaned over and scooped some river water into some of the low places.

Helen demanded, "What? Teacher, what?"

But Annie just answered, "In a minute, Helen."

So Helen was forced to follow Annie's every move with her hands and wait for an explanation. Finally Annie was done. She had built a miniature raised map of the world in mud. Now she guided one of Helen's hands across it as she began to talk into the other.

Annie talked about mountains that burst and burned from their tops. About cities that had been buried under the lava that flowed from these burning mountains. How at one time moving paths of ice had inched down across the surface of the earth, and frozen all forms of life before them. Helen shivered with delicious fear as Annie described the huge monster beasts with their tiny heads and huge bodies who'd battled each other in the mud bogs long, long ago.

Helen learned many difficult things, though she never knew they were difficult. When later she found out that most people considered the earth's own history a series of dull facts, she cried out "No!" in pure disbelief. For to her it had been a magic time, a time of colorful stories and hairbreadth escapes — when Teacher had built up the shape of the world out of Tennessee River mud.

Some of Helen's biggest discoveries weren't about the shapes of butterfly wings, or even the shape of the earth. Perhaps her biggest discoveries concerned herself.

For Helen was barely seven now, and five of those years she'd spent in no-world. She was still woefully ignorant about herself. From the time of her illness, she had never laughed.

One day Annie came tearing into the room, laughing aloud. She grabbed up Helen's hand and, laughing still, let it explore the smiling lips, vibrating throat, and shaking body. At the same time she spelled L-A-U-G-H into Helen's puzzled hand. And then, without a moment's pause for questions, she grabbed Helen, upended her on the bed, and began to tickle her.

Teacher tickled, laughed, and then tickled the squirming child some more. And all the while she was spelling the word L-A-U-G-H.

Suddenly Helen began to smile. Her smile grew broader. A chuckle escaped. Finally with a great whoop, she began to laugh.

Captain Keller and Kate had been drawn to the room by all the noise. Standing in the door for the last few minutes, it had looked to them like a pleasant enough roughhouse — until that sound. Kate put her hands to her open mouth. She drew her breath in sharply, then turned and buried her head against her husband's shoulder.

"Oh, Arthur," she whispered. "I never thought I'd hear that sound from her again. *Helen's laughing!*"

All her life Helen remembered the moment she first grasped an abstract idea. An idea that didn't have a definite size or shape. An idea that she couldn't investigate through her fingers.

It started with Teacher asking Helen a simple question about a combination of numbers. "Helen, if you have a one and two threes, what have you got? How much does that total?"

"S-E-V-E-N-T-E-E-N," Helen spelled back at random.

"No!" Teacher spelled back sharply. "Don't just guess. That's sloppy. Now come on, Helen, and try: one one and two threes. You can do it. Just think."

Helen furrowed her brow. She concentrated on the problem. She tried with all her might.

Just then Teacher leaned forward and tapped her forehead. "T-H-I-N-K!" she spelled at the same time. Suddenly Helen knew that this was what was going on inside her head: *thinking*. Helen savored the new word and the meaning behind it. So that's what she'd been doing. Helen's inner world grew larger.

All of Helen's lessons were not so pleasant. Some, in fact, were downright painful. One day Annie heard an unearthly scream coming from the kitchen, on the first floor. Annie knew it was Helen. "Dear God, what's happened to her?" she thought. Had she hurt herself terribly? She raced downstairs. At the kitchen door she met Mrs. Keller coming from the opposite direction.

But Helen wasn't hurt — just furious. She was in the midst of a temper tantrum, and her anger was directed at Viney, the cook.

"Oh no!" Annie mourned. Helen had been so sweet-tempered the past few months. Now she was tearing and scratching at Viney as if she wanted to destroy her.

Annie pulled Helen away. She tried to soothe the girl by hugging her. But Helen was too excited to respond. So now Annie picked up her hand.

"What's wrong, Helen? Why are you so angry? Tell Teacher." Helen began to cry. And all Annie could pick off her trembling fingers was, "Viney . . . bad. Viney . . . bad!"

"Viney," Annie finally shouted over the continuing din. "What in heaven's name happened here?"

"I don't know," the cook said. "She was filling that

glass with those little round stones she likes to play with, and I was afraid she'd break it and hurt herself. So I tried to take the glass away from her. She tugged and I tugged, and then . . ." Viney made a vague gesture toward the screaming, thrashing Helen. " . . . she started *that*." Viney shook her head.

Annie sighed. She quieted Helen, and then went to her room to think. To think about Helen. Suddenly her mind was flooded with pictures of another little girl. A girl who destroyed things: loaves of bread, her father's shaving mirror, and one Christmas the most beautiful doll in the world.

"If only somebody had cared enough to tell me when I was wrong, and to show me there was another way," Annie thought now. "If only I'd had somebody to be really firm with me when I struck out. *If only I'd had somebody who really cared.*"

Helen came sidling into the room. She crept as close to Teacher as she could, tried to kiss her. Gently Annie held Helen back and spelled into her hand.

"No. Teacher cannot kiss a naughty girl."

"Helen is good. Viney is bad," Helen shot back.

"But you're the one who struck Viney. You kicked her too, didn't you, Helen? You hurt Viney." And then she repeated sadly, "I'm sorry. I cannot kiss such a naughty girl."

Helen stood still for a moment, a flush of red sweeping up her face. It was clear to Annie that a fierce struggle was taking place inside the child. Then Helen grabbed Annie's hand and spelled angrily, "Helen not love Teacher. Helen do love Mother. Mother will beat Viney."

Gently Annie led Helen to a chair and pushed her down into it. "Sit here a while and think, Helen," she said, handing her one of her dolls for company. "Think about what happened. Don't talk about it any more now. Think instead."

The morning passed in separate misery for both of them. At lunch, Annie found she could eat nothing. Helen grew very upset as her hands discovered this.

"Why?" she kept on asking.

"I'm not hungry."

"But why?"

"I'm just not."

"Cook make tea for Teacher," Helen spelled helpfully, and started to climb down.

"No," Annie pulled her back. "My heart is sad, Helen. Too sad for a cup of tea."

Helen began to sob as if her heart would break. Annie relented.

"Poor Helen," she exclaimed aloud. "I'm always pushing you. Forgive me. I should remember you can't learn control in one day. I of all people should know that!" And she pulled the crying child toward her.

"Come, come, Helen." She began to speak into her hand. "It'll be all right. Teacher promises. Let's forget all about this morning for now. Let's go upstairs. I have the most amazing insect to show you. In a jar up there. Come on, it's called a stick bug. We'll talk about it."

So the two of them went upstairs hand in hand. But Annie soon realized that Helen was too full of troubles to fix her mind on any bug.

"Can bugs know about naughty girl?" Helen asked. With a sob, she flung her arms around Annie's neck. "I am good tomorrow. Helen is good all days," she promised.

"Oh, well," Annie thought. "I guess we'll have to push on to the end of the lesson, whether I want to or not. Helen won't let go of it."

So now she spelled, "Will you tell Viney you are very sorry you scratched and kicked her?"

But Helen smiled craftily. "Viney not spell words." Which was true enough. Viney had not yet learned the manual alphabet, so Helen could not communicate directly with her. But Annie would not let Helen off so easily.

"I will tell Viney you are sorry," Annie said. "Will you go with me and find Viney?"

Helen nodded "Yes." So the two of them went off to find Viney. They stood before her, hand in hand. And Helen nodded emphatically as she felt Annie's words of apology being spelled into her palm. She even allowed Viney to kiss her, though she wouldn't return the kiss.

Then, with a deep sigh of relief, she ran upstairs to the bedroom, crawled up onto the bed, and fell immediately into a deep sleep.

Later, Kate and Annie stood looking down at her. "She looks so happy. Let's not wake her up for dinner. You can bring her a sandwich and a cup of milk at bedtime," Kate said.

Annie nodded in agreement. "Yes. The little warrior has earned her sleep. What a battle she won today!"

"And over her own worst enemy, too," Kate added. The two of them left the room, smiling.

Time to Move On

ONE DAY, BEFORE THAT FIRST SUMMER WAS OVER, Annie received a letter from Laura Bridgman. She carried it downstairs with her to read at the lunch table. Before she could finish it, Kate Keller exclaimed, "But Teacher! Helen writes almost as well as that now!"

That was July 31, not four months since Helen had learned the meaning of the word "water." And her amazing progress continued. By the end of August Helen knew 625 words. By October she was writing letters to the little blind girls at Perkins, in Braille. Before the year was out, Annie took her to a circus. Helen asked so many detailed questions about the animals that Annie was forced to spend days and nights finding the answers.

"I feel like a jungle on wheels," she complained, before Helen's curiosity was finally satisfied.

In June of the following year Annie received a letter from Mr. Anagnos, her old director at Perkins. He had been following Helen's progress closely, and he wrote that he would feel deeply honored if Annie would let Helen take part in the graduation ceremonies of the school.

Annie frowned as she read the letter. Was Helen ready to face curious strangers? She had come so far this last year. Was it far enough so that people wouldn't call her an interesting freak? So that they wouldn't pity her too much?

Yes, Annie decided finally. Far enough. Helen could read and write now. She could answer anybody's questions. Their first year of discovery was over. It was time to move on.

Before the month was out, Annie and Helen boarded a northbound train for Boston. When they arrived in the city, they drove directly to Perkins. As soon as Helen had curtsied properly to Mr. Anagnos, she turned to Annie and begged, "Where are the little blind girls? Where are they?" She had been exchanging letters with them for months, and already considered them her dear friends.

Annie laughed. "Come, I'll show you." She led Helen into a large playroom. "They're waiting for you over there." She gave Helen a shove in the right direction, and the little girl ran eagerly into the arms of her new playmates.

The next day Mr. Anagnos asked Annie into his office for a private chat.

"What now for the two of you?" he wanted to know.

"I'm not sure," Annie answered slowly. "I really haven't had time to think much about the future. This past year's been too much of a whirlwind!"

"Annie, have you ever thought of leaving Helen here — permanently, I mean?"

Mr. Anagnos saw Annie frown, so he hurried on. "Oh, and you too, Annie. I wouldn't separate you, never fear. We could find a nice job for you here — teaching the little children, perhaps. You were always good at that."

"Thank you," Annie said dryly. "We shall always be glad of an invitation to visit. We'd love that any time. But we couldn't live here."

"Why not?"

"This morning I took Helen to visit Laura Bridgman.

Helen had been looking forward to it so — she thought they'd be the best of friends because they shared the same handicaps. Do you know what happened? Helen's energy scared Laura to death. She got hysterical when Helen tried to get close to her, and wouldn't calm down until I took Helen away. Why, Laura's whole world is inside that bedroom of hers. Ten by fifteen feet — that's not much of a world. No. This place is too small for Helen."

"Annie, there's just so far you can go!" Mr. Anagnos was sincerely upset. "Helen can never be normal. Don't delude yourself. It can only lead to suffering and heartbreak for both of you. She's *different* . . ."

Annie knew he was genuinely worried. She tried now to answer him.

"I know she'll never be normal. I know she's blind and deaf and dumb, and that sets her apart from others. Oh, yes . . ." Annie's eyes began to shine, ". . . yes indeed. You say she's different from others. And you're right. But I say she's the same. And I'm right too. Inside of herself, behind those handicaps, she's Helen. She's Helen the same way I'm Annie, and the way you're Mr. Anagnos. She's a *person* the same as all other people. So don't worry. We'll be all right. Wait and see!"

The Last Years

THE NEXT FEW YEARS WERE TRIUMPHANT ONES for
Helen and Annie. Helen became more and more
famous as she followed one achievement with another.
In the spring of 1890, she became the second deaf-blind
person in history to learn to speak with her mouth. She
would have to remain blind and deaf all her life, but
she was no longer entirely mute.

When Helen was twelve, she calmly announced, "I

have decided to go to college. And the one I want to go to is Harvard."

Most people felt that college would be impossible for her. How could she hope to compete with seeing and hearing students on such a high level? But there was one person who never questioned her right to try. All Annie said was, "Not Harvard, Helen. That's a boys' school."

In the fall of 1900 Helen entered the freshman class of Radcliffe College. Four years later she took her place in a line of ninety-six girls and felt a rolled-up parchment being placed in her palm. It was her diploma, announcing to all the world that Helen Keller had graduated *cum laude* — with honor — from Radcliffe. She was the best-educated blind-deaf person in the world.

Helen was now a very famous person. Only friends noticed the small woman who always stood at her side. But this never bothered Annie. When a magazine writer asked her to let him write an article around her, she snappd, "No. My life is my own affair." Annie didn't want to be famous. She wanted only to be Teacher.

And so she remained as the years passed. Full years for both of them. Helen became a writer, pouring out books and magazine articles about her life, and later about the problems of the blind and deaf. Together she and Annie toured the United States, giving talks to help people understand the problems of the handicapped.

Finally Annie's amazing energy began to give out. There came the day in the 1920's when she had to say to Helen, "I can't make this lecture trip with you. You'll have to take somebody else along." Helen Keller's teacher was growing old. Worse, she was growing blind.

"Maybe another operation," Annie thought. So she went to a doctor.

"I'm sorry, Annie," he told her gently. "I'm afraid it's the price you'll have to pay for a lifetime of abuse. All those books you read for Helen when you should have been resting your eyes. At least you are fortunate to be specially trained for blindness. With your knowledge of Braille and raised print, you can still read to your heart's content."

"Heart's content!" Annie wailed bitterly. "I hate Braille. I want my eyes. I won't accept blindness. I won't!"

But this was the fight that Annie Sullivan lost. Near the end of her life she became completely blind.

Annie tried to be cheerful for Helen's sake, but one day she complained to a friend, "Smiling is the hardest thing for me to do these days. I'm so furious with this stupid old body of mine. It's become such a lie, with its creaking bones, blind eyes, tiredness. Inside I'm still Annie Sullivan, who can run and ride horses, and stay up day and night without yawning. Inside I can still *see*! Oh, I'm so tired of carrying around this weighty old body of mine!"

"Teacher, don't talk like that!" her friend cried out. You must not leave us. Helen would be nothing without you!"

"Then I would have failed," Annie snapped. For her whole life had been dedicated to making Helen Keller free — free even of Teacher.

On October 19, 1936, Annie Sullivan died. She left Helen to face the hardest adjustment of her life: living without Teacher by her side. Many times Helen felt like quitting. She wanted to huddle in a chair and have people wait on her, have people pamper her with their ready pity. But always a silent voice would prick at her in those moments. "Teacher would not like that, Helen."

So Helen Keller slowly and painfully rebuilt her life into a meaningful pattern. She worked. She laughed. She went on living a full and remarkable life.

Annie hadn't failed.